CORNISH SKETCHBOOK

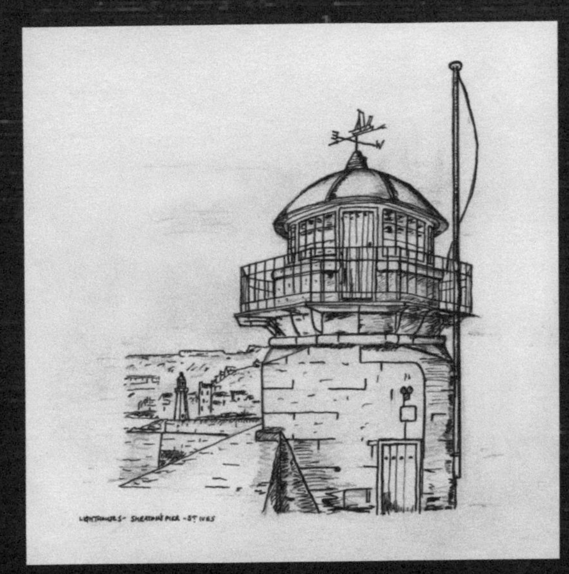

A Tour of West Cornwall

by Graham Sibley

TABLE OF CONTENTS

ACKNOWLEDGEMENTS

My heartfelt thanks go to Hobs Repro of Birmingham, who did such a fantastic job of advising and scanning the original artwork for this book. Their good humour and can-do attitude explain why they are such a success.

My parents and my brother, Andrew, deserve a special mention. Their unfailing support and encouragement for my endeavours made me believe that there might be some merit in the enterprise and, when the energy started to flag, kept me going.

Ultimately, the thanks and credit for this creation must go to my partner Pippa Whittaker for realising my ideas and creating the look and feel of the book. Her unfailing patience in tempering my idiosyncratic use of language has made the descriptions of the scenes within both legible and accessible to those lacking a degree in Sanskrit…

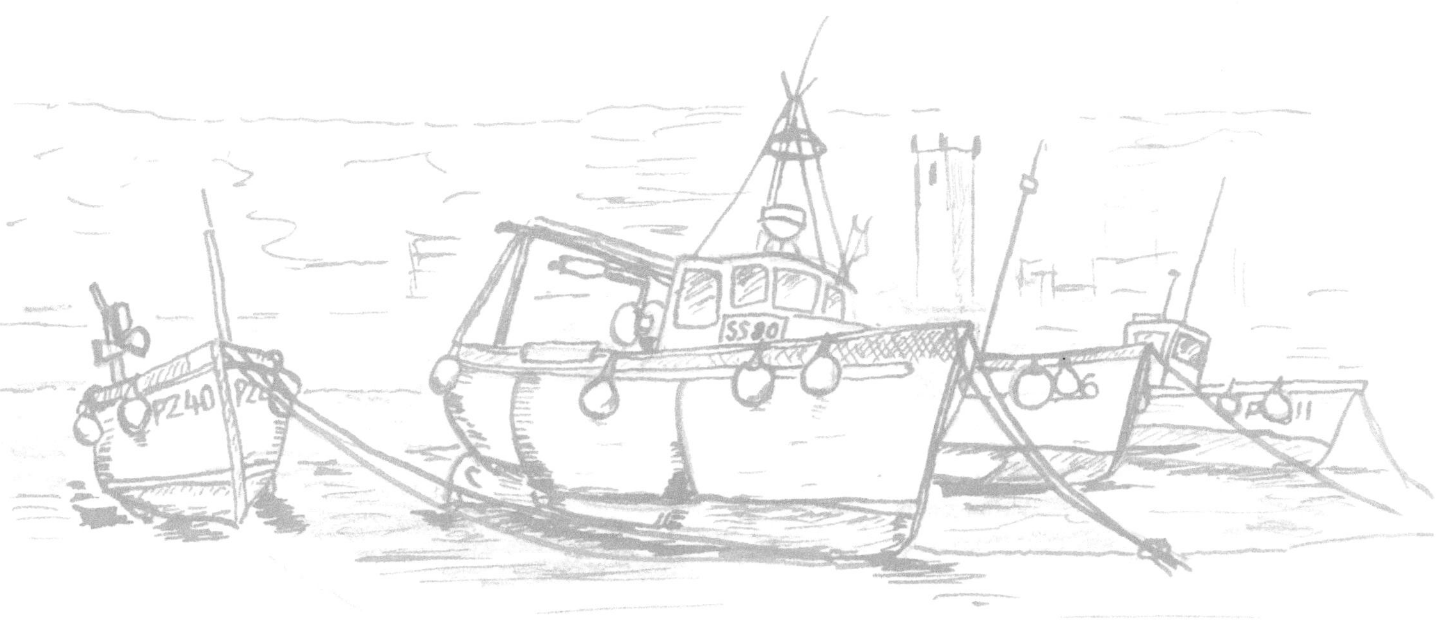

ABOUT THE AUTHOR

Musician, writer and artist Graham Sibley was born and brought up in St. Ives, Cornwall. He attended the local St. Ives schools, and gained the Duchy of Cornwall Scholarship to Gordonstoun School in Scotland in 1985.

Following study at the Guildhall School of Music and Drama in London, he became the Tuba player of Christopher Gable's Northern Ballet Theatre and freelanced with most of the UK's major symphony, ballet, broadcasting and opera orchestras. In addition to commercial recording, he has also performed as a soloist on BBC Radio.

In 2008, he became the Principal Tuba of the City of Birmingham Symphony Orchestra and Birmingham Contemporary Music Group, and has performed with them all over the world. He is also the Tuba teacher at the Royal Birmingham Conservatoire.

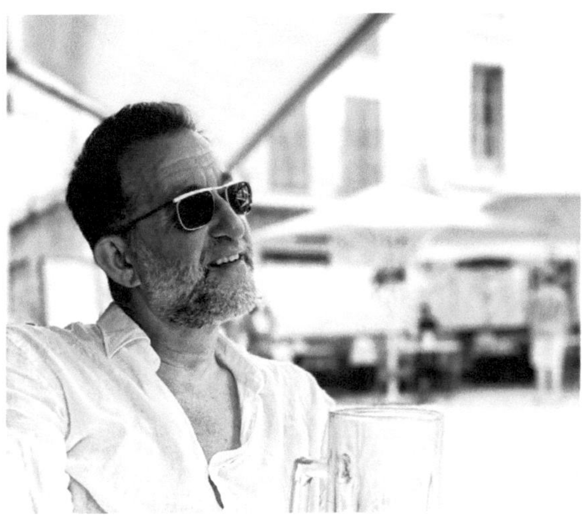

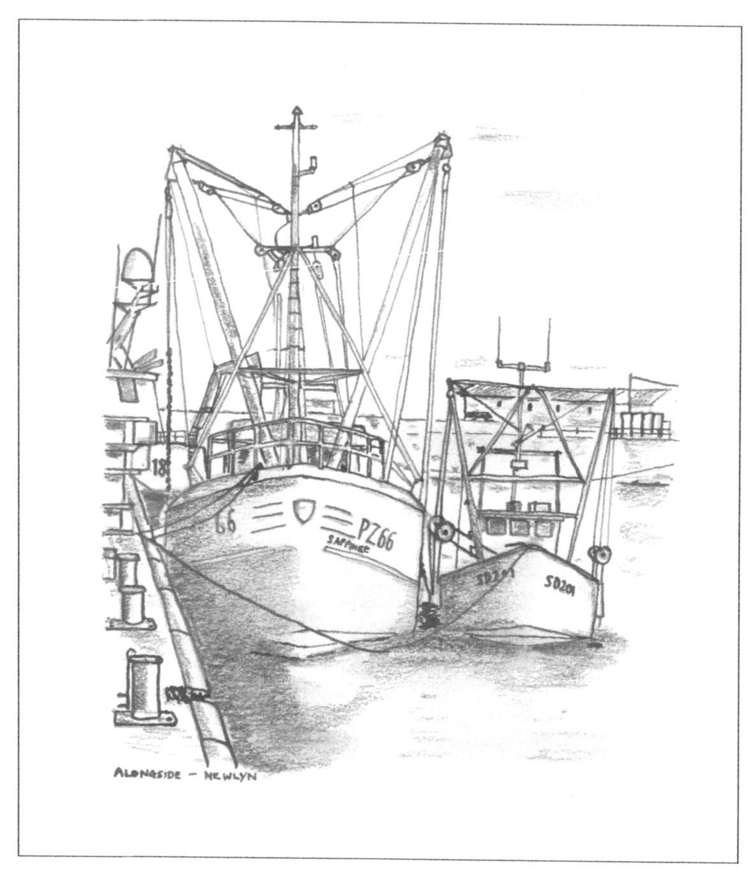

www.pippawhittaker.art

FOREWORD

I was born and brought up in St. Ives, and though I've not lived there for many years, I still regard both it and the surrounding area as my home. It's not simply that my family is there, or that there are memories and familiar sights at every turn. It goes deeper than that. It's a feeling of belonging to it somehow, of being part of an experience or timeline that stretches off in either direction beyond a single lifespan.

This book loosely and personally describes the Penwith Peninsula from St. Ives Bay to Mount's Bay. As a family, we must have explored every part of it on dog walks, car jaunts, school trips and brass band engagements when I was growing up. It is rich with memory and experience.

Visually, it is substantially unchanged within living memory, and I suppose therein lies its enduring appeal for people to visit it year after year. After all, in a world where everything appears to change at dizzying speed, it is profoundly comforting to return to somewhere that is the same as you left it - is it not?

Once a thriving area of fishing and mining, it has now softened into a landscape marked by ancient monuments and industrial relics. Despite its apparent wildness, it is shaped by the unmistakable hand of man as much as by nature, and the two have commingled to create a place as fascinating as it is unique.

These drawings make no pretension of great art, but what they attempt to convey - along with the descriptions and personal anecdotes - is my deep, enduring attachment to the place. If it draws the reader into a greater understanding and empathy for this remote part of the world, then it will have done what I intended it to do....

GODREVY LIGHTHOUSE, GWITHIAN, ST. IVES BAY

Built in the late 1850s and acting as a sentinel for the treacherous Stones Reef, which heads out in a straight line from it, the octagonal towered Godrevy Lighthouse faces the full fury of the Atlantic on the edge of St. Ives Bay.
The Stones Reef had long been a hazard for shipping, but it was the loss of the Steamer 'Nile' with all its crew and passengers in 1854 which finally provided the catalyst for Trinity House to build a lighthouse on this small desolate island, which first shone its light five years later, in 1859.

Manned by two keepers, who worked two months on and one month off, it was supplied by boat from St. Ives. Godrevy was automated as early as 1934, and now its only frequent visitors are sea birds and a colony of grey seals. It's no surprise that it was automated as early as it was (the lighthouses around Lands End weren't fully automated until the 1980s) because I recall a trip on my father's boat around the island one summer. The landing stage is to the back of the island, and its harsh sheer concrete and rusting ladders and derricks made for a forbidding sight - even in a gentle swell. The idea of jumping from a pitching boat onto a ladder with the breakers clawing at you is not an appealing one!

This was the light that inspired the Virginia Wolf tale 'To the Lighthouse' and its isolation, close to the coast, makes for an arresting sight. The Woolf family were regular visitors to the area and rented Talland House in St. Ives from family friends. 'To the Lighthouse', though set in Scotland, relies heavily on Woolf's adolescent experience, and much of the descriptions clearly depict St. Ives Bay and its lighthouse.

In terms of local folklore, it was told to me that a local fisherman - whose appropriate sobriquet was 'Health & Strength'- swam from St. Ives Harbour to here and back for a bet in the 1950s...no small feat that as it's a round trip of seven miles!

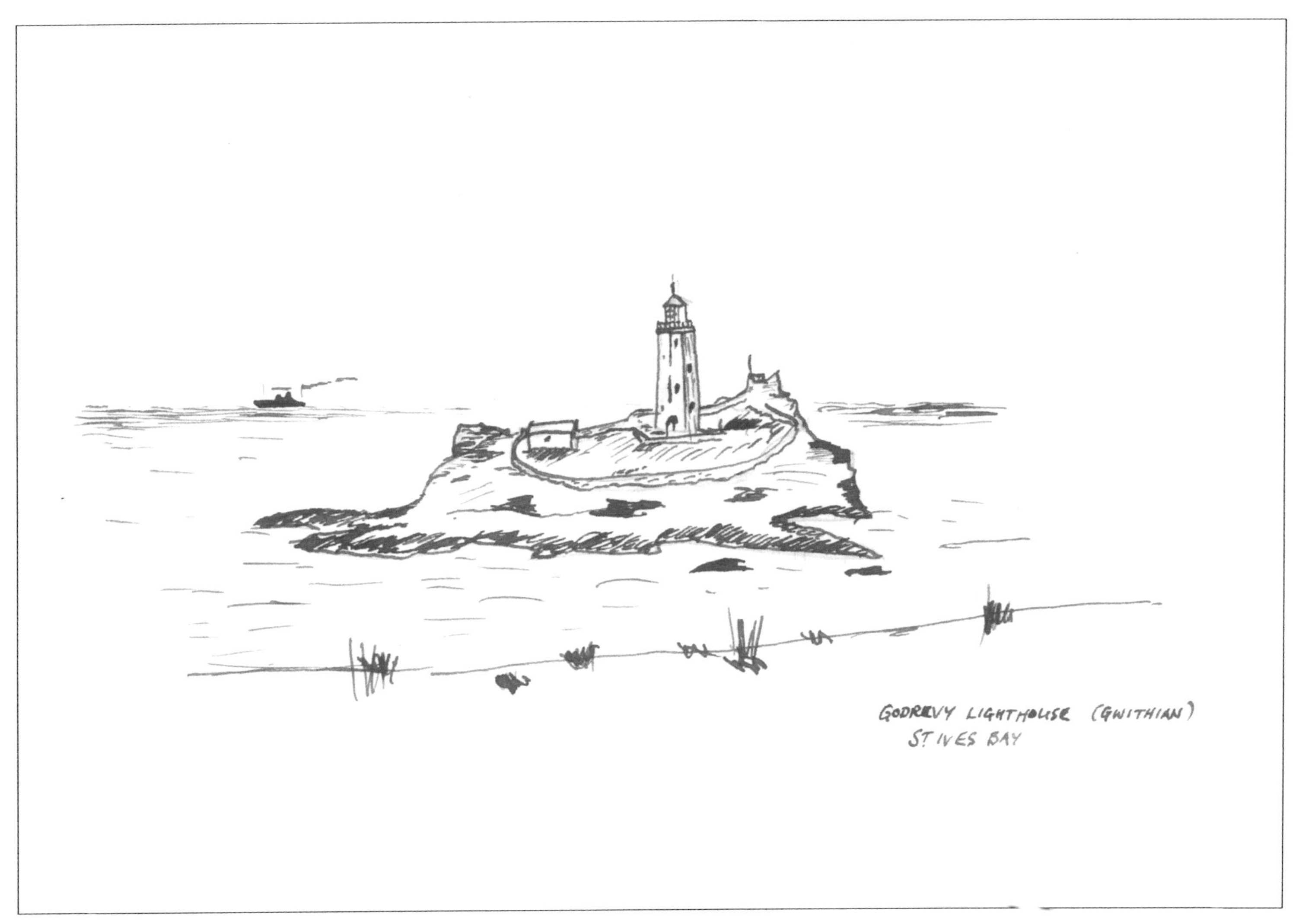

GODREVY LIGHTHOUSE (GWITHIAN)
ST IVES BAY

THE ST. IVES BRANCHLINE, PORTHKIDNEY

"Starlings on the chimney pots,
And gulls are on the sea,
And all is gay in Carbis Bay,
And that's the place for me."

So goes the local song that celebrates a chaotic family excursion on this, quite possibly the most spectacular branch line in the UK. For most of its four-mile length, it hugs the cliff tops and sand dunes along the edge of the Hayle Estuary and St. Ives Bay and offers dramatic views of the whole area in all weathers.

Built in 1877, it was the last line to be built in the broad 7ft gauge and was pivotal in transforming the town into the world-renowned artistic and holiday destination it has become. In its heyday, 10 carriage trains would arrive directly from Paddington to St. Ives - reversing at St. Erth - in the guise of the 'Cornish Riviera Express'. How civilised that must have been!!

Astonishingly, the line only narrowly escaped closure in the 1960s due to the personal intervention of the then transport minister Barbara Castle: a decision proved prescient now that the line does so much to reduce road congestion into the town during the busiest months of the year.

As a boy, my grandparents would take me on the train from St. Ives to St. Erth as a special treat, and I would sit behind the driver's partition in rapt childish attention with my nose pressed to the glass to see the line winding ahead. When you board at St. Erth, sit on the platform side of the train for the best views…it really is the best way to get to St. Ives…

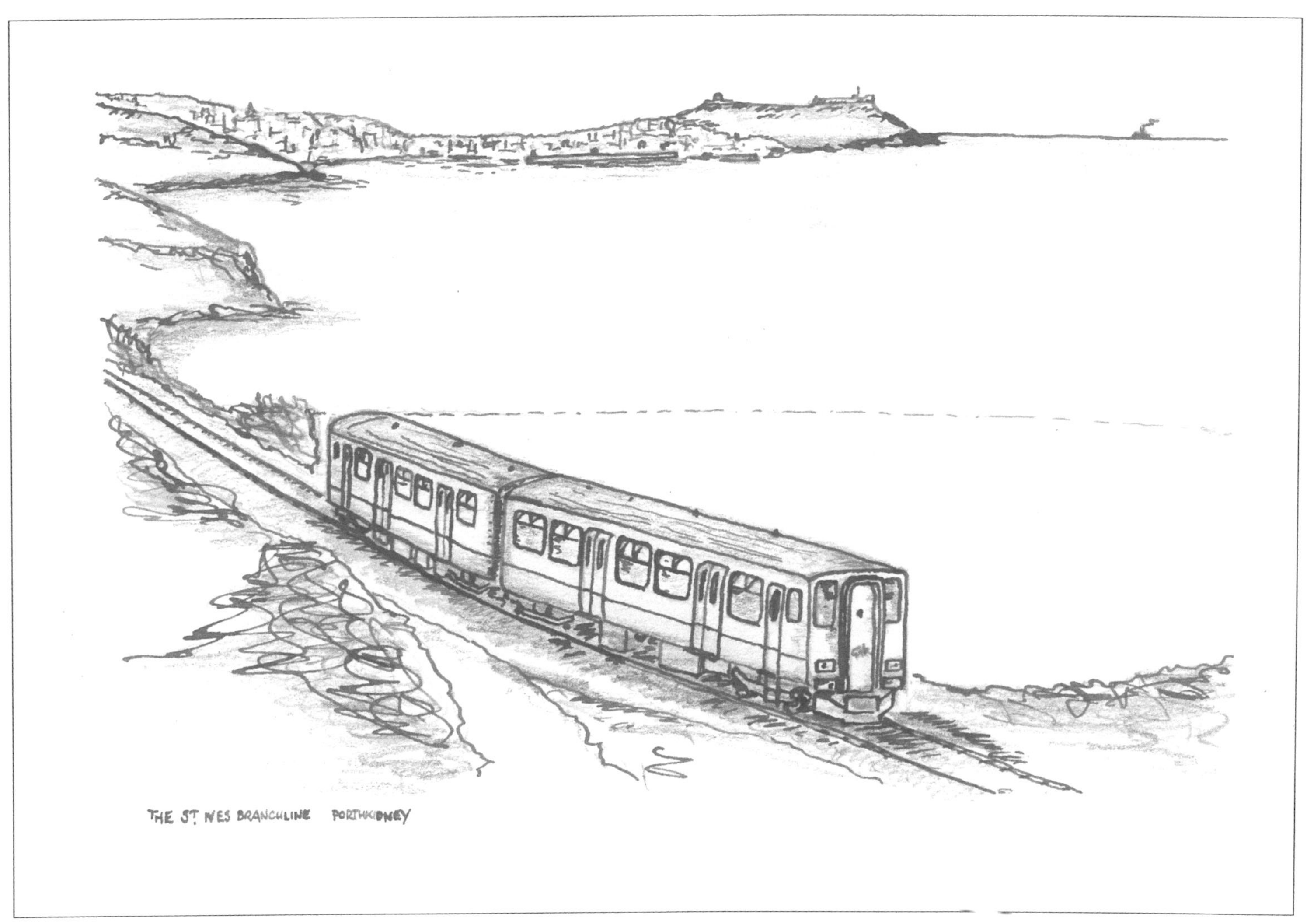

THE ST IVES BRANCHLINE   PORTHKIDNEY

MARKET PLACE AND PARISH CHURCH, ST. IVES

This is the central hub where all roads in the town eventually lead. The oval building was originally home to the town council and the Magistrates Court before the completion of the Guildhall on Street An Pol in 1939.

My Dad remembers working on the roof here in the early 1970s and seeing the Magistrate's chair still dustily holding court in the upstairs chamber! Now, its ground floor is the home to a variety of art and clothes shops, and you have to be careful as to which way the traffic is coming from when you emerge from them (traffic priority seems to change arbitrarily from year to year!)

The Parish Church of St. Ia is the 'high church' presence in the town and dates from the early 1400s. It's dedicated to the town's namesake saint, who allegedly paddled over from Ireland in a coracle or a giant leaf in the 5th or 6th centuries to convert the still heathen Cornish, landing here in St. Ives. I can't imagine that - even fired with missionary zeal - this was an easy undertaking!

It's a typical sturdy Cornish granite-built church with a squat buttressed tower and three aisles which closely resemble the Parish Church in Lelant. I'm told that in style, it's more Devonian than Cornish. Inside, in the Lady Chapel, is a statue by Barbara Hepworth and in the Churchyard, a late medieval lantern cross...

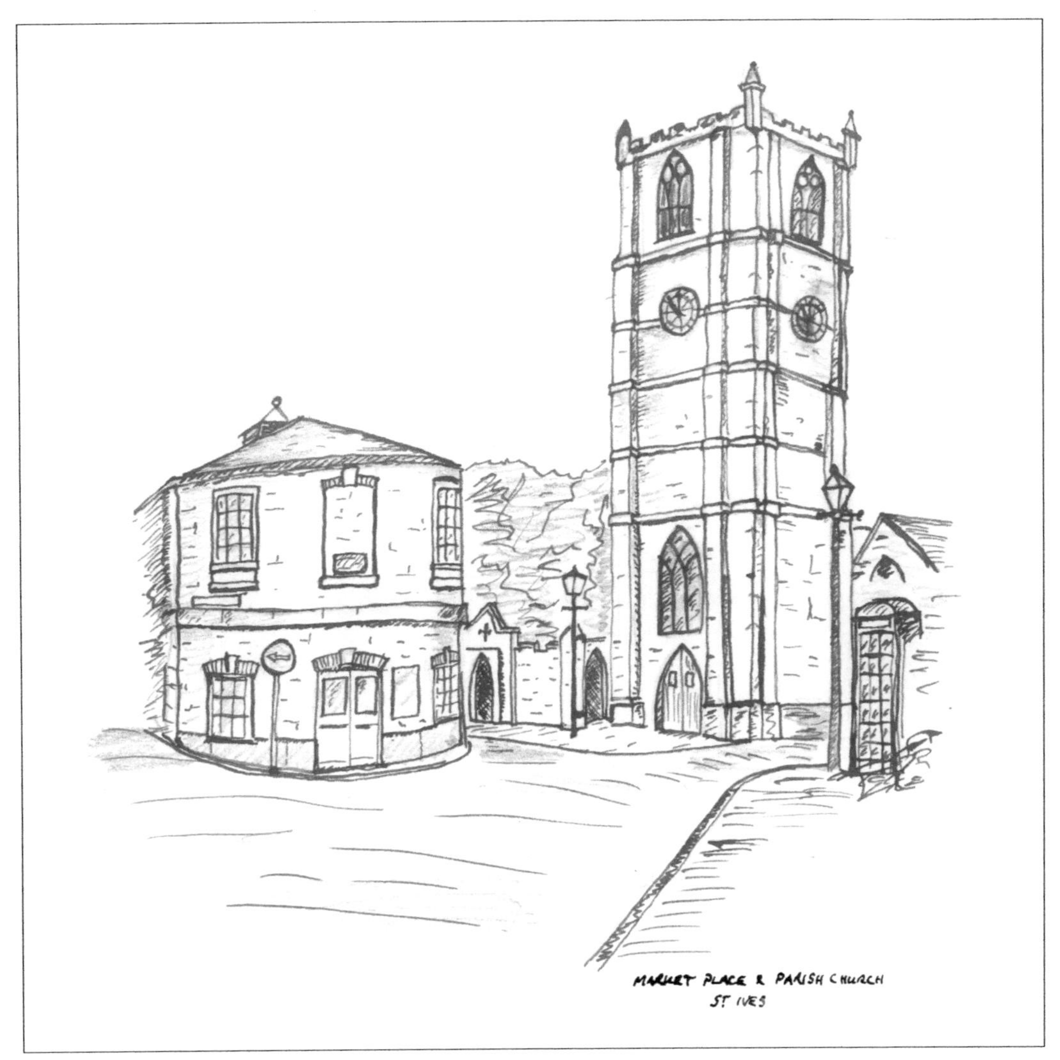

MARKET PLACE & PARISH CHURCH
ST IVES

THE LIFEBOAT STATION, ST. IVES

It's amazing to think that, even now, the Royal National Lifeboat Institution is funded by public subscription and is not a state supported-body. To consider that each lifeboat is crewed mainly by volunteers (only the Coxswain and engineer are paid) makes the whole arrangement even more remarkable.

Anyone who has stood on the coast in the full fury of a storm or gale can appreciate the overwhelming power and might of nature unleashed. To see a huge vessel violently thrown about at sea or grinding and breaking up on the rocks is a sobering and timely reminder that we are powerless in the face of nature. To be the kind of individual who willingly sets out in just such conditions to aid others must therefore require particular heroism and fortitude that few will ever be required to find within themselves.

The St. Ives lifeboat has a long and proud history, rich in its share of heroism and tragedy. In 1938 the lifeboat was lost when it was smashed on the rocks while rescuing the crew of the SS Alba close to the Island at St. Ives. A year later, only one member of the crew survived a further disaster when the lifeboat 'John and Sarah Eliza Stych' capsized several times in another rescue. The fact that the current Coxswain of the St. Ives lifeboat is the great great grandson of the Coxswain who died in that disaster, and also the son of a later highly decorated Coxswain, says much of the tradition and sense of duty that runs through both this station and the RNLI as a whole.....

The current lifeboat moved across the wharf to its current location in 1994. Prior to this, it lived next door to the Salvation Army citadel on, appropriately named, Lifeboat Hill. The boat would be drawn on its trailer by a crawler along the wharf and down the slip onto the sand if it were low tide - and this would always generate much excitement. It also made the boat slow to launch, so - when the old Princess Royal was retired and replaced by a larger, more modern boat, a new lifeboat house was needed, and a slipway was built in front of it at right angles to the West Pier....

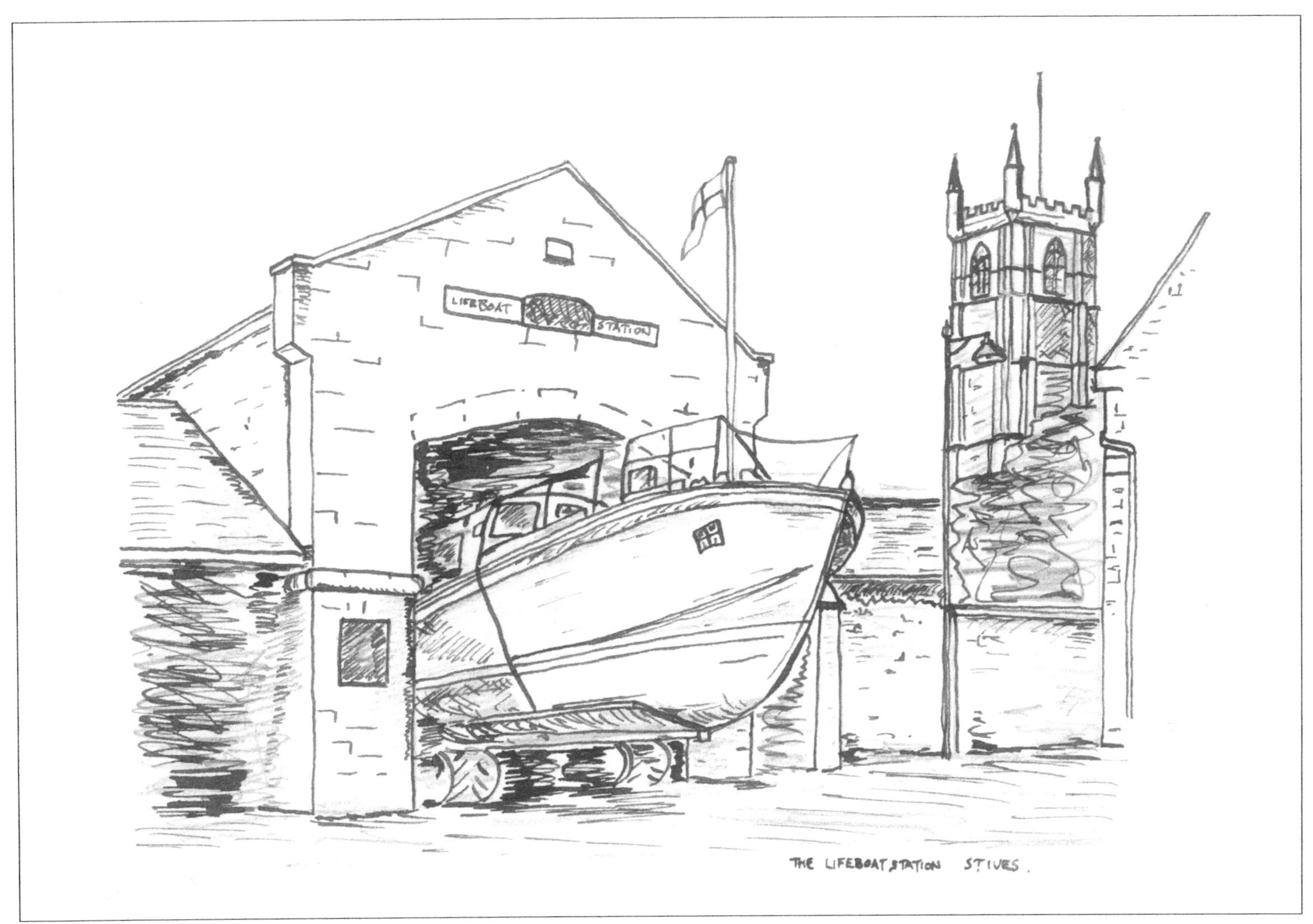

THE LIFEBOAT STATION ST IVES.

FORE STREET, ST. IVES

The main shopping street of the town, Fore Street, is rarely quiet, and during the summer, when thronged with tourists, it can be quite a challenge to negotiate its narrow, cobbled confines.

This view is taken from what was the entrance to the old Woolworths shop and looks back down towards the Market Place and Parish Church. Down on the right, are two pubs quite close together - The Union Inn and The Castle Inn. The Union has a fantastic selection of pictures of old St. Ives by the bar. The Castle became the favourite watering-hole of the post-war arts community, being frequented by such luminaries as Barbara Hepworth, Ben Nicholson and Peter Lanyon, to name but a few. It is told that on some evenings, the ale-fuelled artistic debate could get a little heated!

If you turn through 180 degrees, it's a short walk along this delightful street to emerge at the harbour on the wharf across from the slipway and next to The Sloop Inn.

Nearly all of the shops I remember as a youngster are long gone. Only two remain - The St Ives Bookshop at No.2, and Leddra Chemist at No.7. But I can remember all the others very clearly: Emjems on the corner; Stephen's The Newsagents; Turners the Electrician's; Leddra's the Chemists; Whites the Furnishers; Hollows the toy shop (linked to 'The Boathouse' on the wharf); Woolworths; Simpson's Gentlemen's Outfitters (here a shop assistant had allegedly seen a pair of suit trousers walk down the stairs by themselves!). The list goes on…

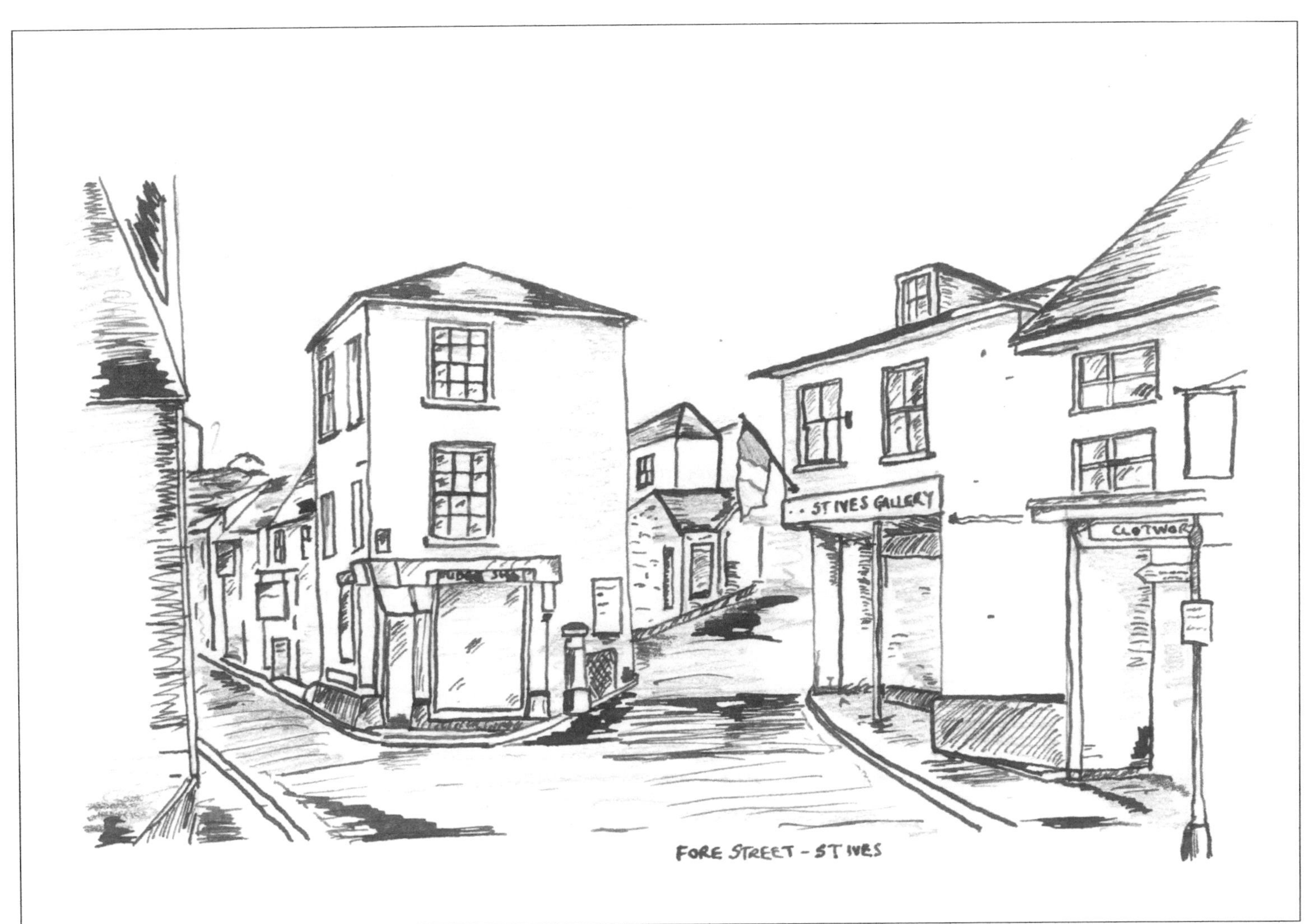

FORE STREET - ST IVES

KNILL'S MONUMENT (THE STEEPLE), ST. IVES

John Knill was a customs collector (1762-1782) and Mayor of St. Ives (1767-1782), and he was, by all accounts, something of an eccentric. There's a shop about two-thirds of the way along Fore Street that, until recently, bore his name - 'Knill House', and this was his home.

The 49ft high granite steeple is built on the summit of Worvas Hill above St. Ives and was originally intended to be Knill's mausoleum. Sadly, it was not to be, but in his will, he bequeathed a sum of £25 to be spent celebrating his life, every five years, on 25th July - which is St. James' Day. John Knill Day - as it is now known in the town - has been celebrated without interruption since 1801 and is one of the UK's oldest local ceremonies. A fiddler in full 18th century dress provides the accompaniment for a procession of the Mayor, Vicar and ten white-dressed maidens, from the Guildhall up to the Malakoff Gardens. This sight gets even more bizarre, when the gathering makes its way up to the Steeple, and the Mayor and Vicar solemnly waltz with all ten local girls around the monument's base!

The Steeple is surrounded by woods, and one emerges at the summit to enjoy spectacular views across the bay, and on a clear day, over much of the locality in near complete tranquility. It was not an area that I had cause to visit frequently, but one family tradition was a Sunday morning trip up to the nearby Trenwith Woods to gather moss. My parents had vibrant geranium hanging baskets around the house, and as a preparation for planting, these were lined with moss. The whole family would head up to the woods (the dog too!), and we'd disperse to scrape the lush growth from the stones and rocks that littered the woodland floor into bags to reconvene later and compare our harvest! I always found this departure from the usual family walks along Porthkidney or Gwithian an exciting deviation, being very different from the usual routine and always unexpected….

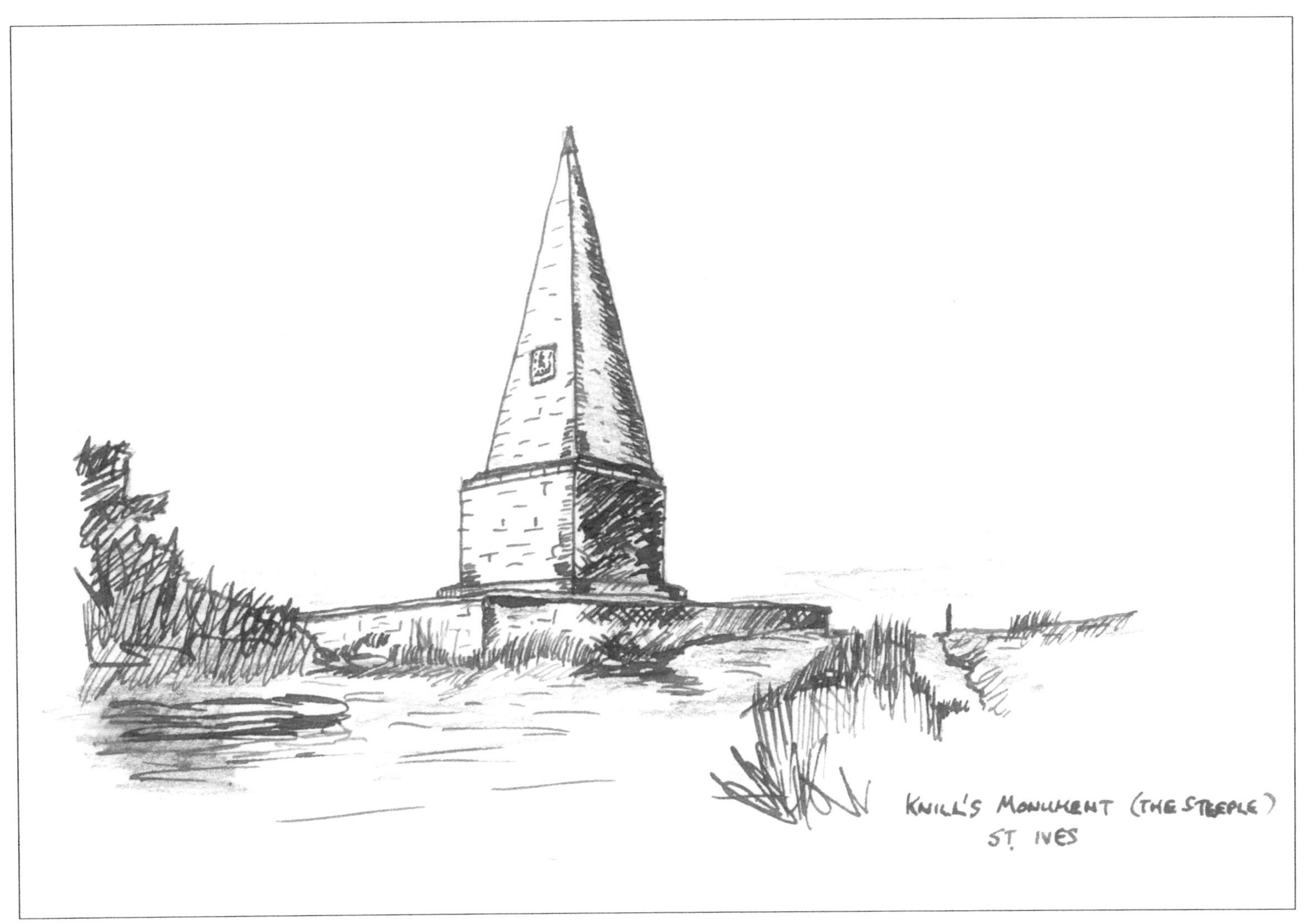

KNILL'S MONUMENT (THE STEEPLE)
ST. IVES

THE DIGEY, ST. IVES

This famous street is thought to derive its name from a corruption of the Cornish 'Dye-Chy' or Dye House.

It's supposed that at some point in the very distant past, there was just such an establishment here that would have dyed the sails for the local fishing boats - though nothing is recorded to support this assertion.

Halfway along its length is a peculiar free-standing granite arch that marks the entry into Hicks Court. There's a plaque stating "This arch marks the entry to Hick's Court where stood the house of George Hicks, Portreeve, 1611 and 1624."

If you are coming down Fore Street towards the harbour - The Digey is the first street allowing vehicular access across the old town to Backroad West and Porthmeor beach.

Riding my bike along it at any speed was a tooth-loosening experience on the cobbles - and it could be alarming to be caught halfway along with one of the local taxi drivers hurtling heedlessly towards you in his Austin Cambridge!

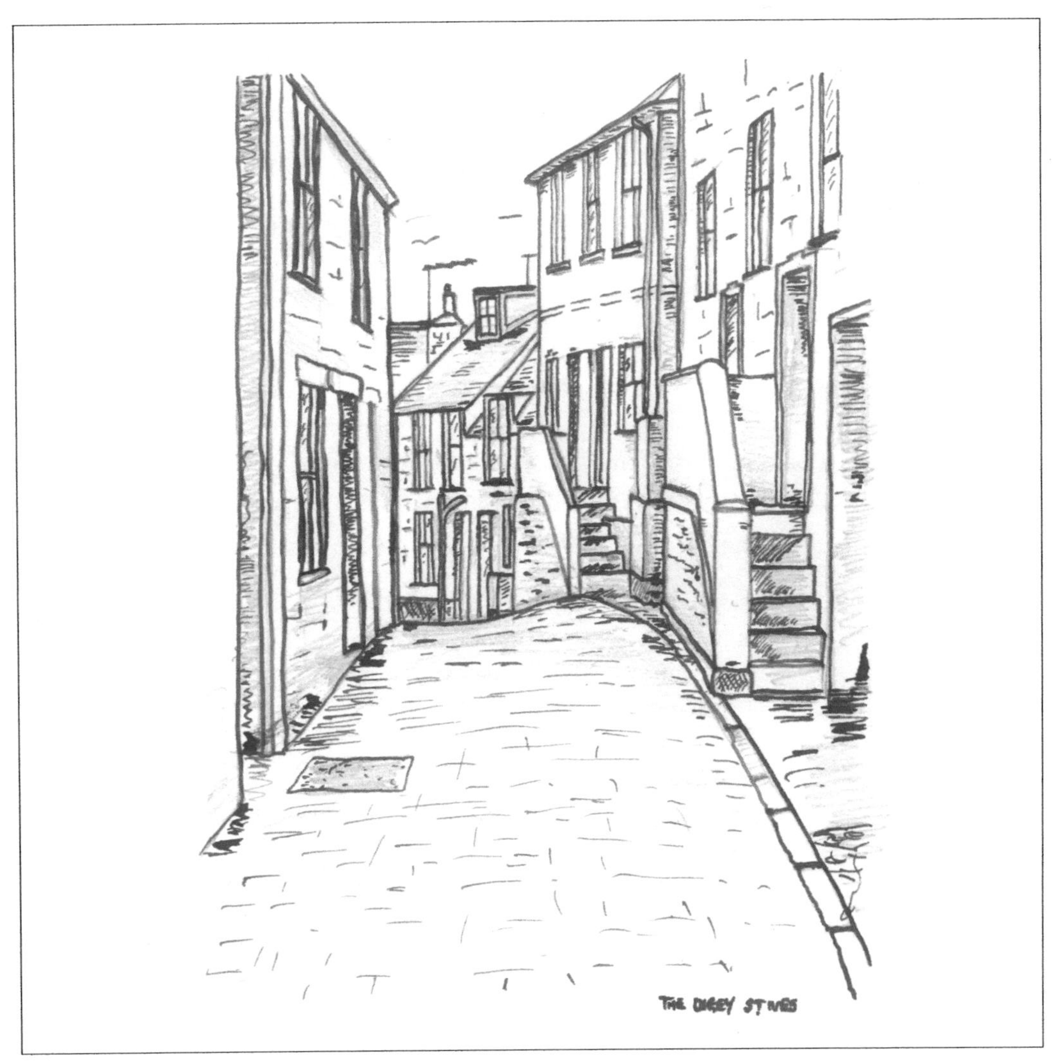
THE DIGEY ST IVES

BARNOON HILL, ST. IVES

Apart from arriving by sea, there is almost no way of getting out of the oldest part of St Ives without negotiating some pretty steep hills!

My family used to live in Ayr, and this is reached by some of the steepest hills in the town. Bullens Lane used to be a challenge for the buses to Nancledra and Penzance. Windsor Hill was a single-track horror that felt almost vertical as you walked or drove up it. Porthmeor Hill is deceptive with a sharp turn revealing a precipitous ascent that regularly unsettled the unwary holiday motorist giving rise to frantic grinding gear changes and desperately harrowing handbrake starts. The weary tread of sunburned beachgoers on their way back to Ayr Holiday Park after a day's basking was a feature of the summer months…breathless owners and soggy, panting dogs of the winter ones.

Barnoon Hill leads down from the Cemetery (where 'naïve' style painter Alfred Wallis is buried) and up to Ayr. At the top, it passes the back of a fine Victorian terrace that has the most splendid views over the town and St. Ives Bay. This view down the hill is popular with painters as it shows the Parish Church standing above the jumble of rooftops and Porthminster point in the background.

The bottom of the hill is transected by Ayr Lane, which leads down to Fore Street on the left and a long wearying drag up to Windsor Terrace on the right. The Barbara Hepworth Museum and Sculpture Garden is on the corner.

It was a regular dare to free-wheel down this hill, oblivious of any potential traffic coming from left or right, with the added thrill of trying to stay in the saddle when you met the cobbles at the bottom!

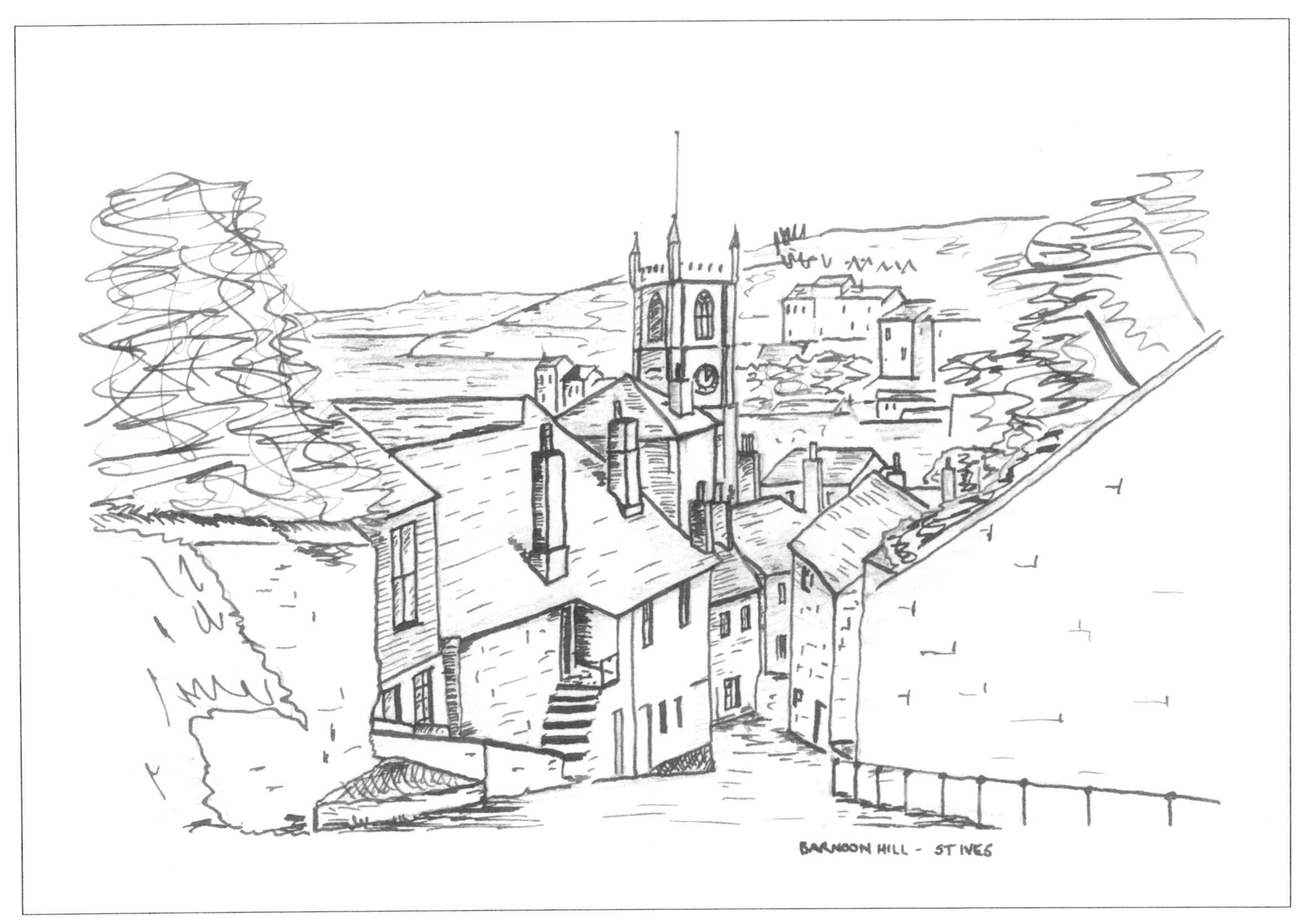

BARNOON HILL - ST IVES

THE HARBOUR, ST. IVES

Once one of the main fishing ports in England, the St. Ives pilchard fishing fleet has dwindled to a handful of active boats. Only a few remain in the harbour all year round and these tend to be much smaller than the deep sea variety found over in Newlyn.

Nonetheless, the harbour is an endlessly inspiring setting for artists of all media and skills, and because of this, it is probably the most reproduced and iconic of settings in the whole of the west country.

In almost all but the most inclement of conditions, it is rare indeed to wander across the beach-quality sand at low tide and not find someone with a sketch pad, easel, or camera engrossed in capturing an arresting play of light on the stonework or the flow of lines of a beached fishing boat…..

Pictured here are a couple of the working boats - SS80 was for a while my father's boat and was maintained with the love and meticulousness that all of his boats have been. Its apple green paintwork and rich varnished gunnels were given an almost mirror-like finish, and its mechanicals were no less thoroughly maintained.

Though not named by him, it retained its original name Didi II (Dydee Two) which - purely by coincidence - was the affectionate nickname my grandfather had always used for my mother - Didi.

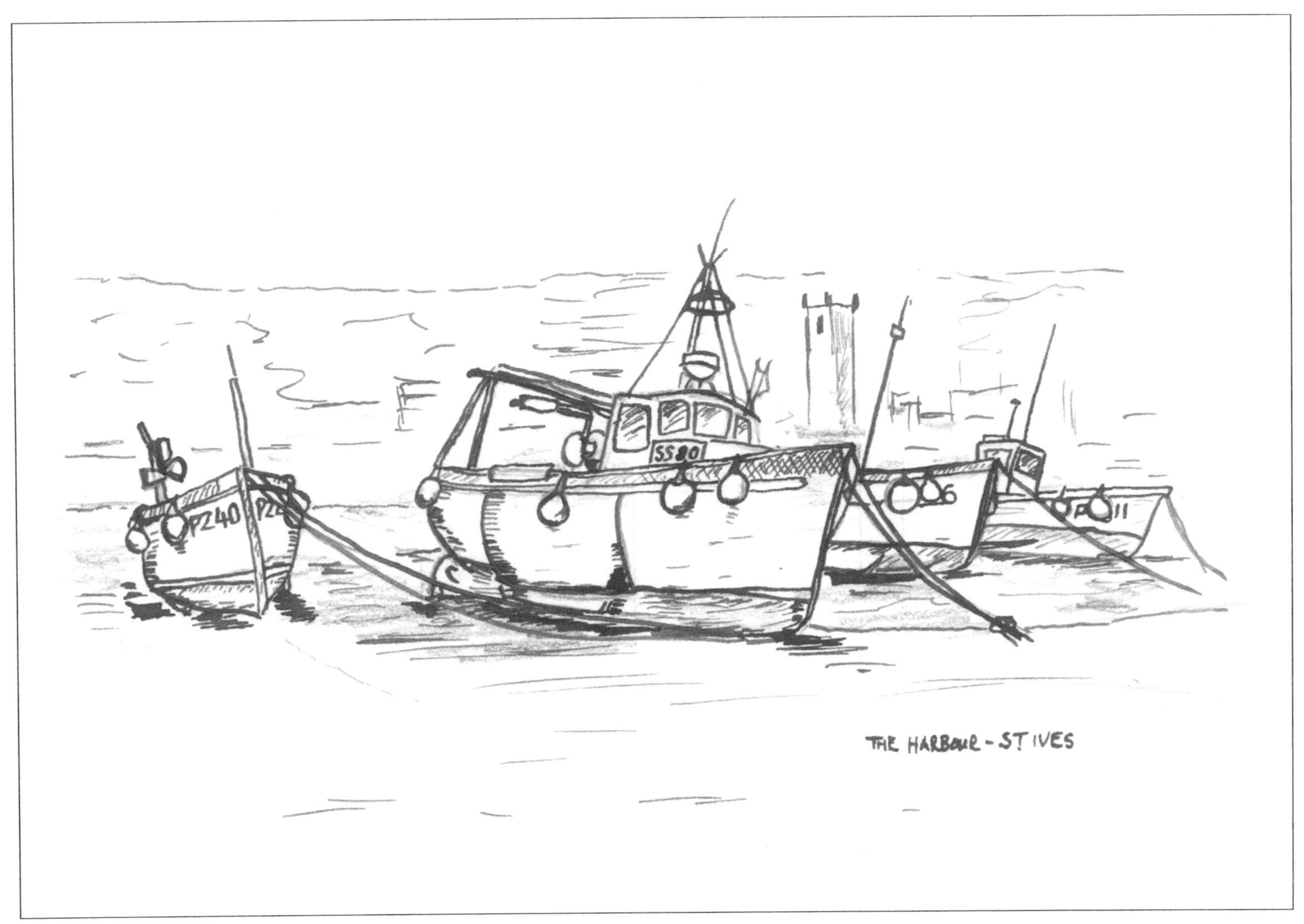

PZ40
SS80
PO11
THE HARBOUR - ST IVES

SMEATON'S PIER, ST. IVES

The two main quays in St. Ives (oddly called piers) are the short 'West Pier' next to the Lifeboat Station and the longer and older 'Smeatons Pier'.

Smeatons Pier is named after its builder John Smeaton who is much more famous as a pioneering lighthouse builder and engineer. His groundbreaking 1759 Eddystone Lighthouse (the third of such!) is familiar to all as the monument on Plymouth Hoe.

The two lighthouses on this dog-legged shaped pier give it an unmistakable silhouette and both have become iconic symbols of the town. Why two? The original pier was extended in the 1890s, making the squat central granite lighthouse redundant. It has been used as a fisherman's store pretty much ever since.

The three arches at the landward end of the pier are a notable feature and always excite interest. Their function is to act as a tidal sluice and prevent the build-up of sand and silt in the harbour. The tide swirls in a clockwise fashion, and the pier forms a barrier - the arches making an outlet for this natural motion.

Above can be seen a short section of railway which was for the original crane to move to and fro when the baulks of timber needed to be removed or replaced. Now long gone, a mobile crane is summoned when required. I recall that for a few years it was deemed unnecessary to service the tidal sluice, but old wisdom and practice was eventually proved when the sand built up to within a couple of feet of the arch ceilings, and you could step off the wharf onto the harbour sand with little trouble!

When I was young, I can vividly recall seeing the local fishermen mending their nets on the quay: threading and sowing…

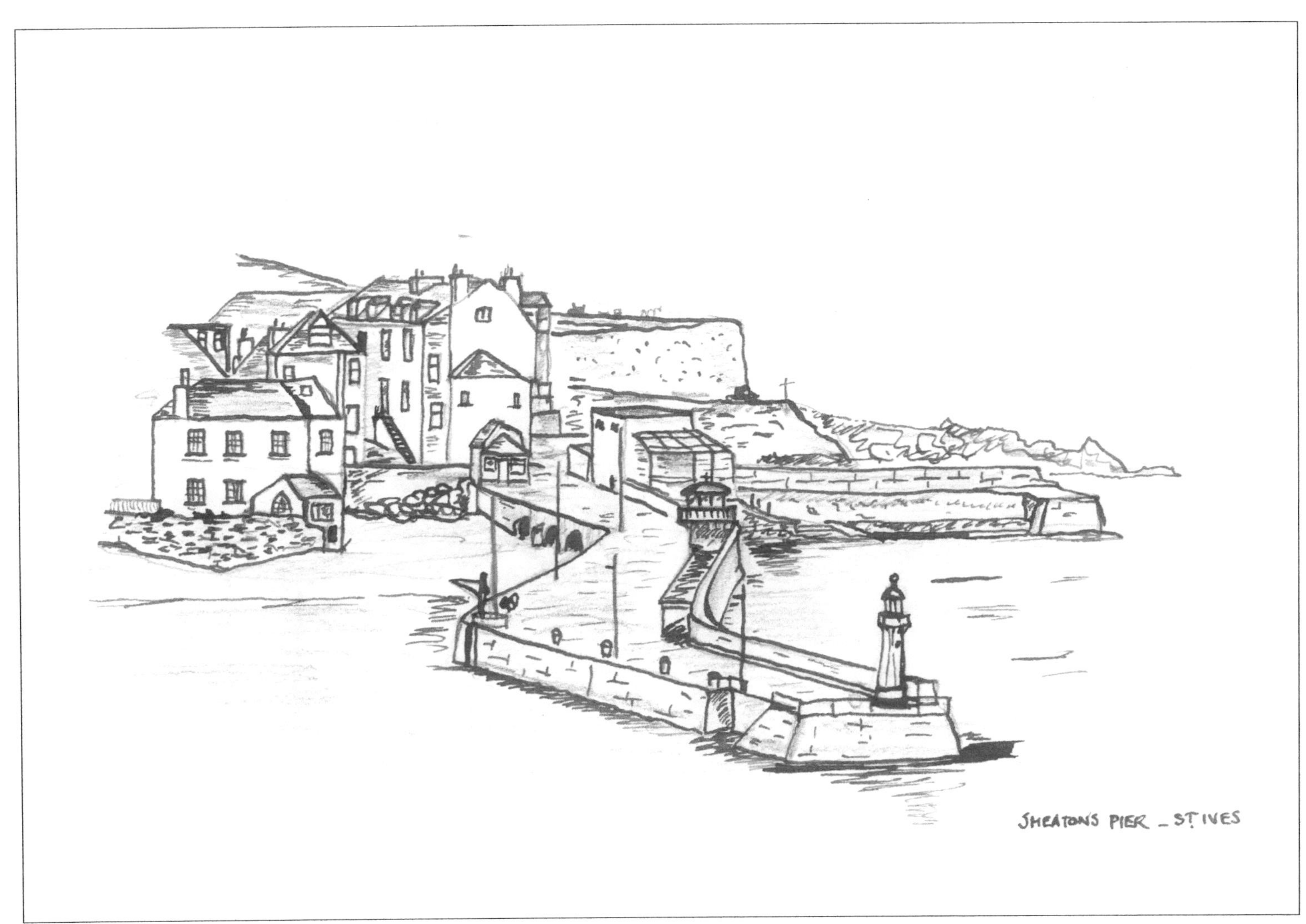

SMEATONS PIER _ ST IVES

SS49, ST. IVES

Typical of many of the older boats that I remember in St. Ives, most of these are now lost to time. With their wooden hulls and larger crews, these former drifters and seine boats were both costly to maintain and labour intensive to operate.

All of which proved their undoing in the 1970s and '80s when the local fishing industry started to really struggle with the combination of competition from Europe, dwindling inshore fish stocks and increased fuel costs after the first oil crisis.

These were sturdy craft and stood up to decades of heavy use and the merciless attrition of the Atlantic weather - as did their crews…

Most had disappeared by the late 1980s, and now you'd be hard pressed to find a boat like this as anything other than a rotting hulk or a converted houseboat in a quiet creek over on the River Helford or the Fal…

"Well Cornish lads are fishermen,
And Cornish lads are miners too,
But when the fish and tin are gone,
What are the Cornish boys to do?"

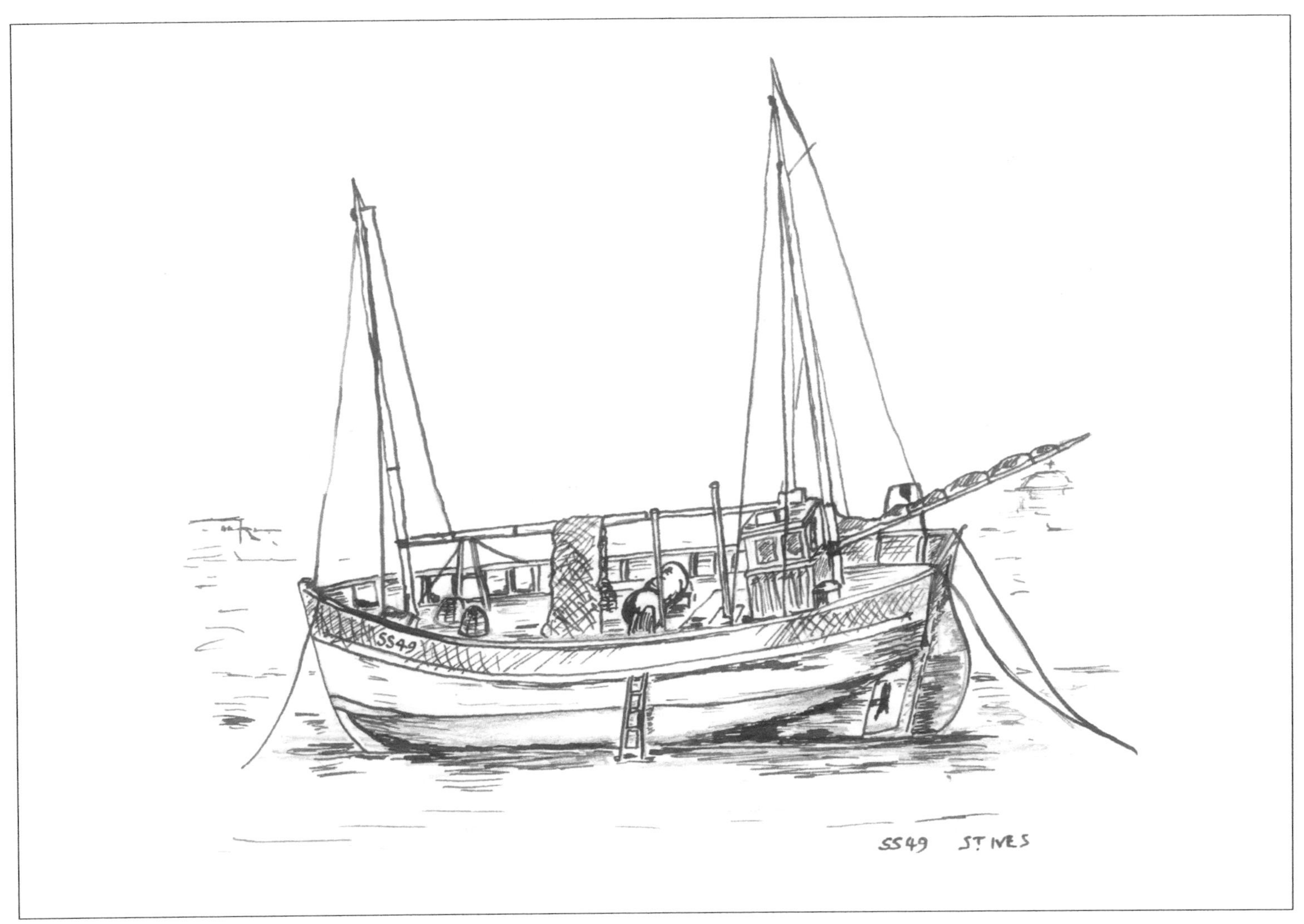

SS49
SS49 ST IVES

THE SLOOP INN, ST. IVES

Situated in the prime location on the wharf adjacent to the slipway, 'The Sloop' has been the fisherman's watering hole since the early 1400s. It is one of the oldest buildings in the town - the oldest being a cottage just around the corner on Fish Street.

Its low-beamed ceilings and black painted benches make for a cosy and welcoming cocoon in winter and a cool respite from the sun's glare in summer - when it can get very busy indeed. On the walls inside, along with the usual assorted nauticalia, are a selection of pencil portraits of local fishermen from the 1940s and 1950s. These are by the artist Hyman Segal who captures his subjects with wit and sensitivity…

The Inn hasn't escaped an appearance or two on the silver screen either. It was used in a memorable scene from the film 'Raise the Titanic'. Within its rustic interior, Sir Alec Guinness (the last surviving officer) takes a White Star Line pennant from its display case and presents it to the salvagers. I recall this filming in the area with vividness. Many local people were used as extras - the grave diggers up at Barnoon Cemetery were even authentically employed as…grave diggers!!!

Out the back is the car park and this was once the site of 'Pudding Bag Lane' (in one end and out the same - according to local speak!) which, as the description suggests, was built in a loop. It's astonishing to think, that before its demolition in 1939, such a small area contained so many cramped homes.

Before he left St. Ives, my brother spent his summers and more than a few Christmases working as a barman here - returning nightly with local tales of goings on….

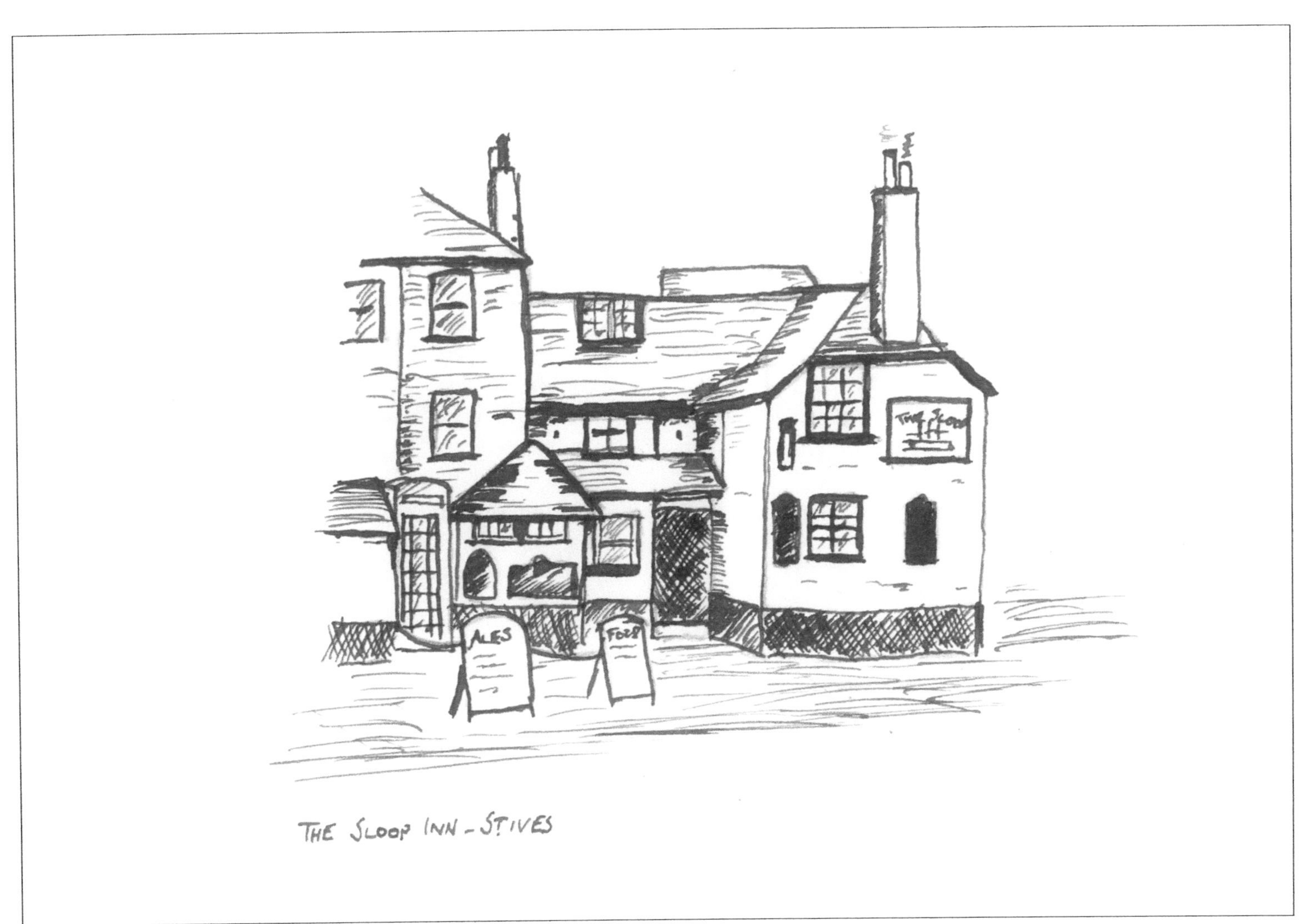

THE SLOOP INN - ST IVES

LIGHTHOUSES, SMEATON'S PIER, ST. IVES

The two lighthouses on Smeatons Pier are emblematic. If a poster or instantly recognisable representation of St. Ives is required, one or both of the lighthouses will suffice to make the observer immediately aware of the location.

From postcards to posters, or tea towels to gin bottle labels, the old granite lighthouse is to be found; and with it the distinct imaginary whiff of the sea, the stoic endurance of a seaward life of honest toil, or perhaps just the sun-kissed memories of happy holidays....

Myths perhaps, but harmless ones, because in the end this squat, now redundant lighthouse is an appealing building in and of itself and encourages any and all to make an image of it.

For nearly 150 years, it has served as a fisherman's store and has weathered storms for another 100 more than that. I suppose that time and the elements have combined to create a thing that is no longer solely of man's design and thus its enduring appeal.

It has always provided a perfect diving point from the quay for those keen to do so, and though prohibited, we would regularly do so at high tide as youngsters. You had to be careful if you timed your jumping sessions wrongly and the Harbour Master spotted you, because a fearsome admonition would be delivered - and, as he knew all of our parents - we all knew that a second helping would await us on our return home if we didn't make ourselves scarce!!!

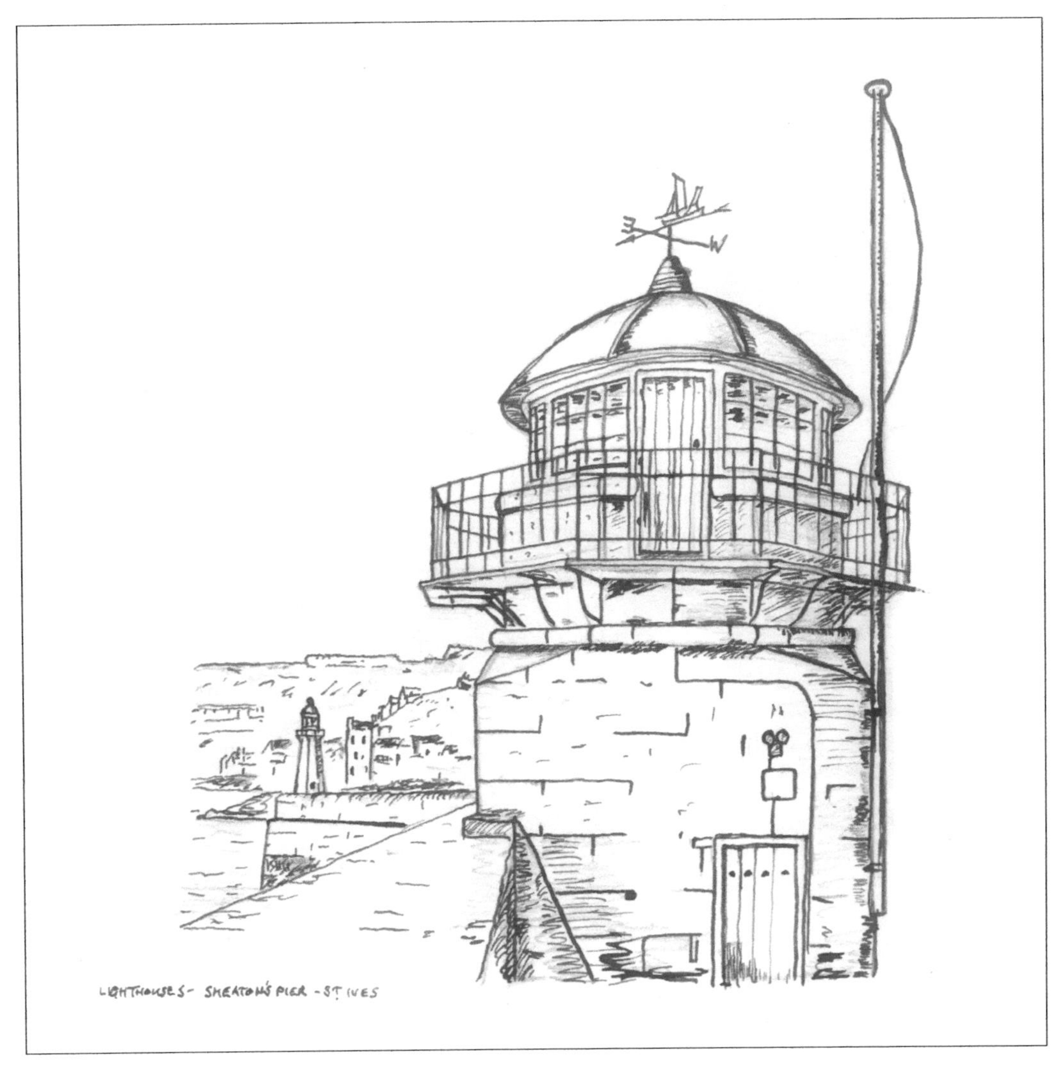
LIGHTHOUSES- SMEATON'S PIER -ST IVES

THE HARBOUR 2, ST. IVES

This is the fishing fleet I remember as a small boy. The assorted collection of converted sailing luggers, drifters, and seiners. All had enigmatic names - Castle Wraith, Purity, Trasbar, Resolve, or similar. Rare was it for a boat to be christened with a family name - presumably because it would be bad luck…

I can recall the banter and sometimes the quiet concentration of the fishermen as they would mend their nets on the quay in fine weather (I can just about remember my Dad doing this in a faded and paint-spattered traditional smock on Smeaton's Pier!)

Despite the number of boats and the crews that manned them, the writing was already on the wall for this way of life. Economics, ecology and politics meant that in less than a generation, much of what you see here would have gone from St. Ives. The newer, more serviceable boats went over to Newlyn, and the older ones quietly languished on the salt flats over the bay in Lelant.

This demise had a predictable script. The boat would be tied up and covered. Gradually these covers would succumb to the weather, and the boat beneath would be exposed to the ravages of the seasons. Eventually, after one of the periodic annual storms, an ageing rotten timber would 'give', and the sea would begin its reclamation in earnest.

Thereafter, the end was relatively swift, and before long, all that would remain would be a few weed-encrusted ribs poking through the mud at low tide - an old dead sea beast, long forgotten….

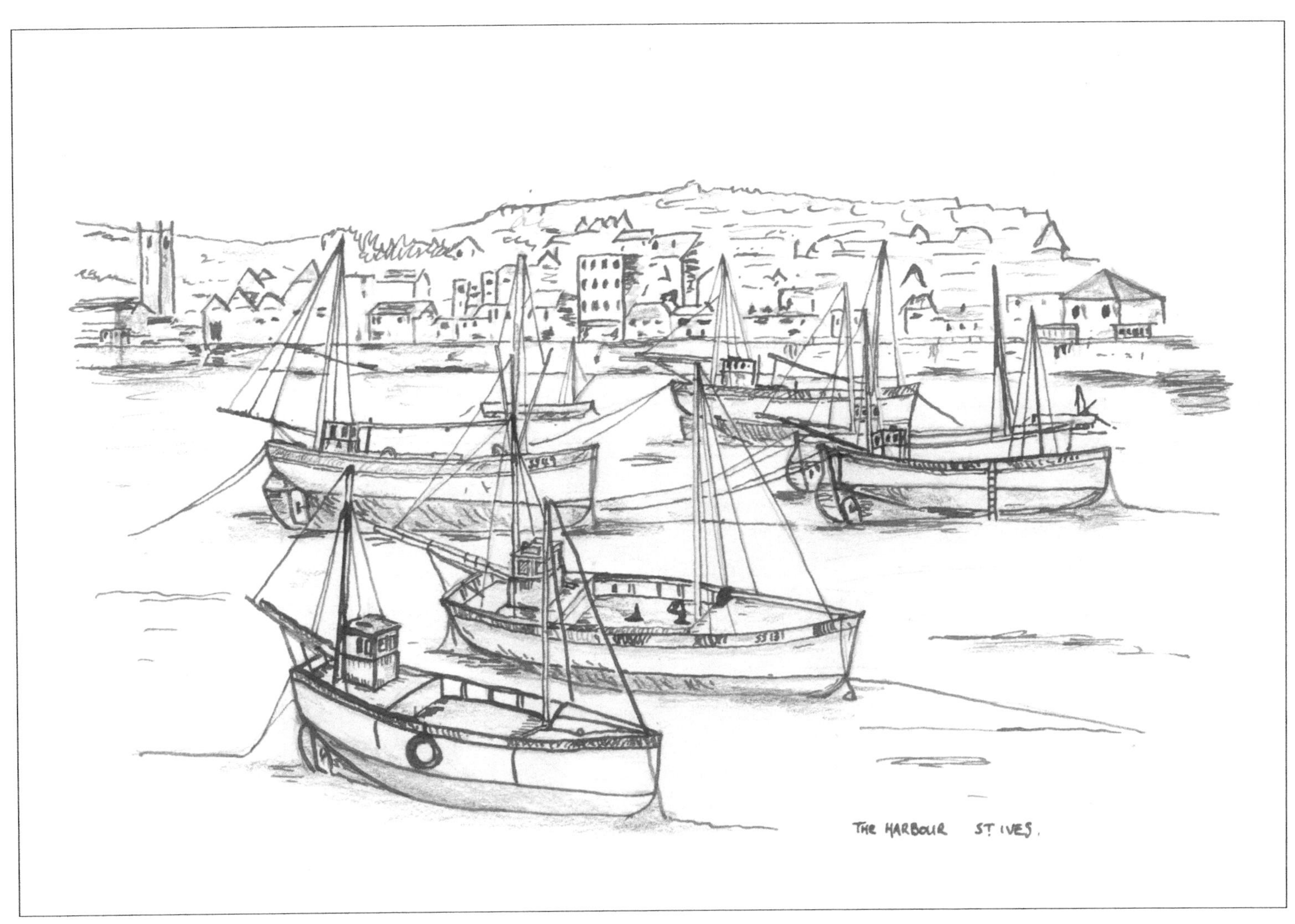

THE HARBOUR   ST IVES.

THE LIGHTHOUSE, SMEATON'S PIER, ST. IVES

The cast iron lighthouse at the end of Smeaton's Pier has a lonely feel to it. When you stand on the seaward side of the quay (where the buttress stops), you suddenly feel very exposed, and the town and harbour feel a long way away…if you're standing there alone, it almost seems as if you're on a boat and out to sea.

At the foot of the lighthouse, and on the corner of the pier, is an old capstan and two pulley wheels which were used in the days of sail to warp the larger sailing boats and visiting ships around the pier's end in a calm. These were still useable when I was young but have now been abandoned to nature and the elements. Rusty, decayed, abandoned and encrusted, they seem ancient.

Not so the lighthouse, which was spruced up and painted not so very long ago. It was built when the pier was extended in the 1890s and consequently has a much more functional form compared to its sister further up the pier. It is also taller and thus less appealing to jump into the water from! The light within and the opposing light across on the West Pier are the marine identifications for St. Ives.

Originally, the light on the West Pier was blue and was unique in the Western Hemisphere. I recall an almighty storm in a teacup that was played out in the local paper - 'The Times and Echo' - when Trinity House decided to modernise and change it to two red lamps one above the other!

Returning to the harbour after a fishing trip, it is always a welcome sight as you round the end of the pier……

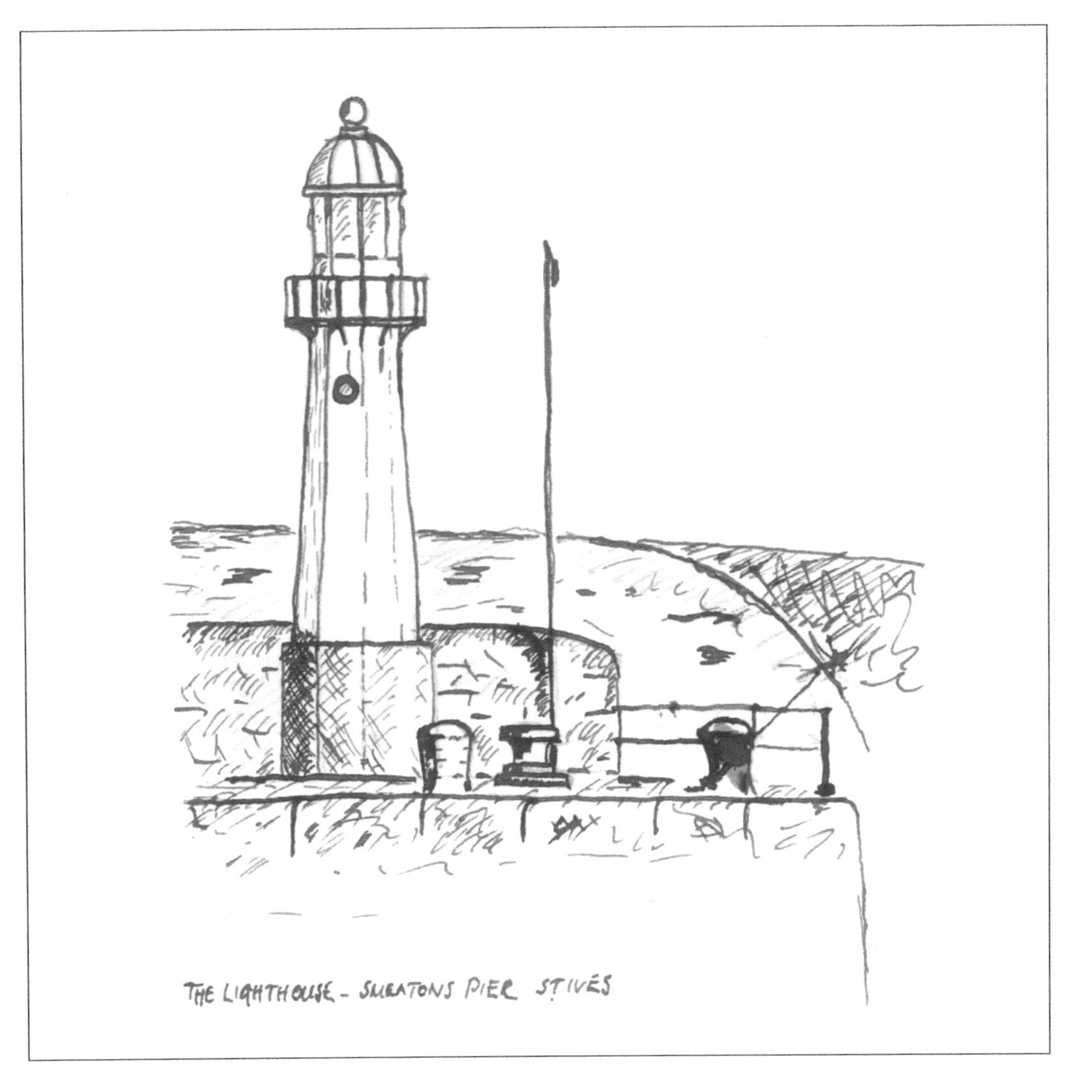

THE LIGHTHOUSE - SMEATONS PIER ST IVES

SHIPWRECK, HMS WAVE, WESCOTT'S QUAY, ST. IVES

You will need a largescale map to see and appreciate the sheer number of shipwrecks that line the Cornish coast. There are an estimated 6,000 of them, and the number of souls who have perished along this coastline must run into the tens of thousands. Though the practice of wrecking (using a beacon to lure ships onto the rocks and loot their cargo) had been stamped out by the end of the 18th century, the combination of storms, human error and a treacherous coast meant that shipwrecks were all too common right up to the advent of radar and latterly GPS. Mercifully, fatal shipwrecks are now rare but as late as the 1980s - and as the infamous Penlee disaster showed - a combination of mechanical failure and a ferocious storm can still claim lives.

Royal Navy wrecks are rare, but within the space of a few years, Cornwall saw two dramatic occurrences: the Battleship HMS Warspite, which broke loose twice whilst being towed to the breakers in 1947; and the one pictured here - HMS Wave in 1952. HMS Wave, a 1,000 tonne minesweeper, was sheltering in St. Ives Bay from a gale and broke her anchor chain. Before she could raise steam, she was driven ashore on the Lambeth Walk beach by Wescott's Quay, and her 62 crew had to be rescued by breeches buoy. Though nobody was seriously injured, it was a dramatic rescue. There is Pathé newsreel footage of the wreck and its later salvage on YouTube!

Though this event was some time before I was even a twinkle in my father's eye, I do remember seeing several shipwrecks as I was growing up: one, a coaster at Land's End lying on its side with the sea boiling around its twisted upper works; and one particularly notable event where both a cargo ship and its rescue tug ended up beached across the bay on Porthkidney Sands and Gwithian respectively.

To walk around something as huge as an ocean-going ship flung onto a beach like a child's plaything is an awe-inspiring experience, and a timely reminder that we are only the masters when nature and circumstances permit!

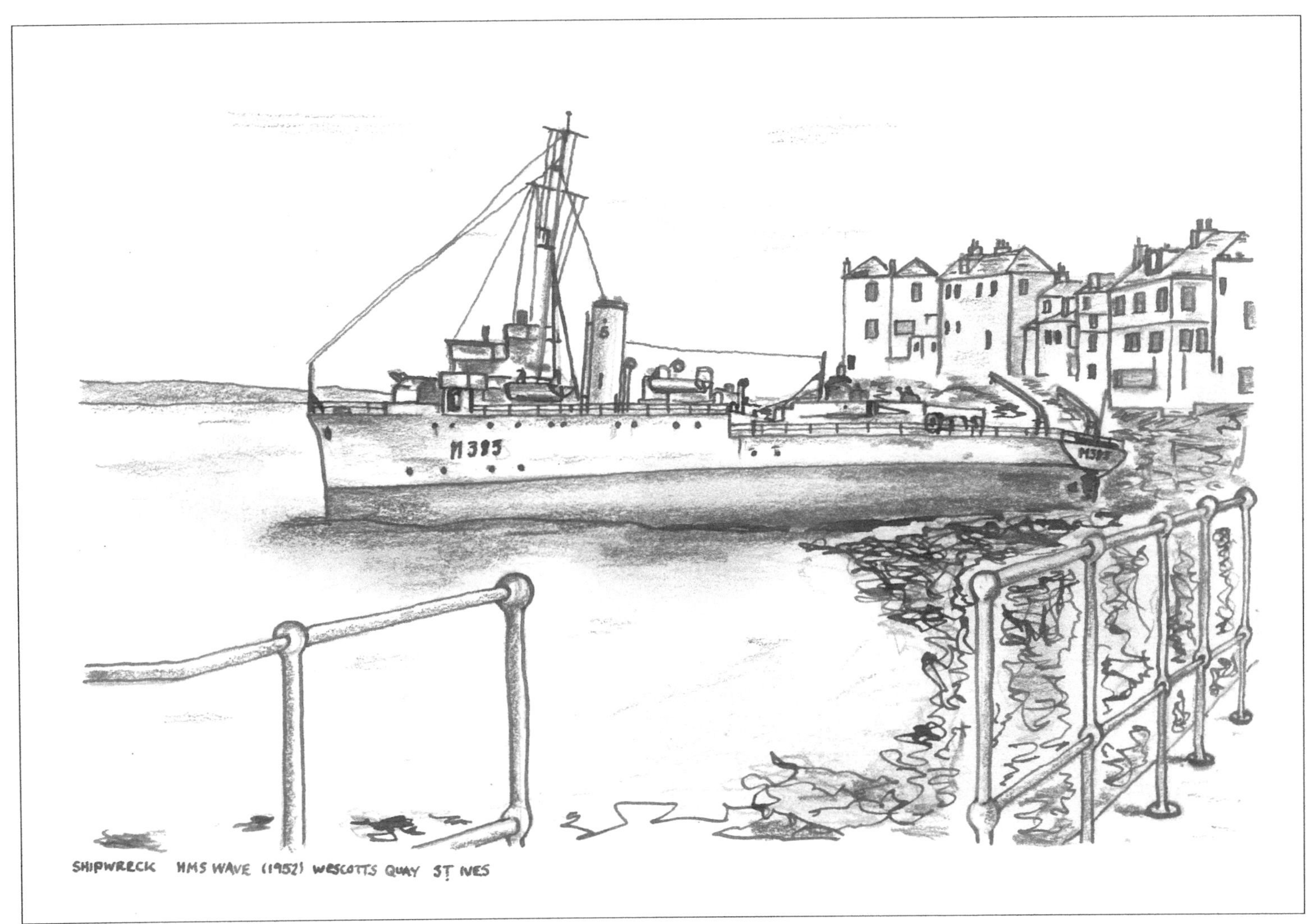

SHIPWRECK   HMS WAVE (1952) WESCOTTS QUAY   ST IVES

BAMALUZ, ST. IVES

Tucked away between the harbour and Porthgwidden, and sheltered beneath the remains of the Wheal Dream tin mine, Bamaluz is a quiet spot even when the town is at its busiest.

Only really accessible via steep rocky steps at low tide, it tends to disappear altogether during spring tides, but it is, nonetheless, a hidden gem at all others - especially when it catches the morning sun. It's also the only all-year dog-friendly beach in the town!

Rampers Pier in the background is the stone part of a short-lived, 19th century wooden jetty, the remains of which can be seen on the lowest tides. It's not unusual to spot an inquisitive seal or even a dolphin close by.

Here, large excursion boats could disembark passengers at pretty much any state of the tide and, for a while, I do remember the 'Seal Island' trips (on board the Cornish Queen and Cornish Belle) would leave from a short walkway laid alongside these remains.

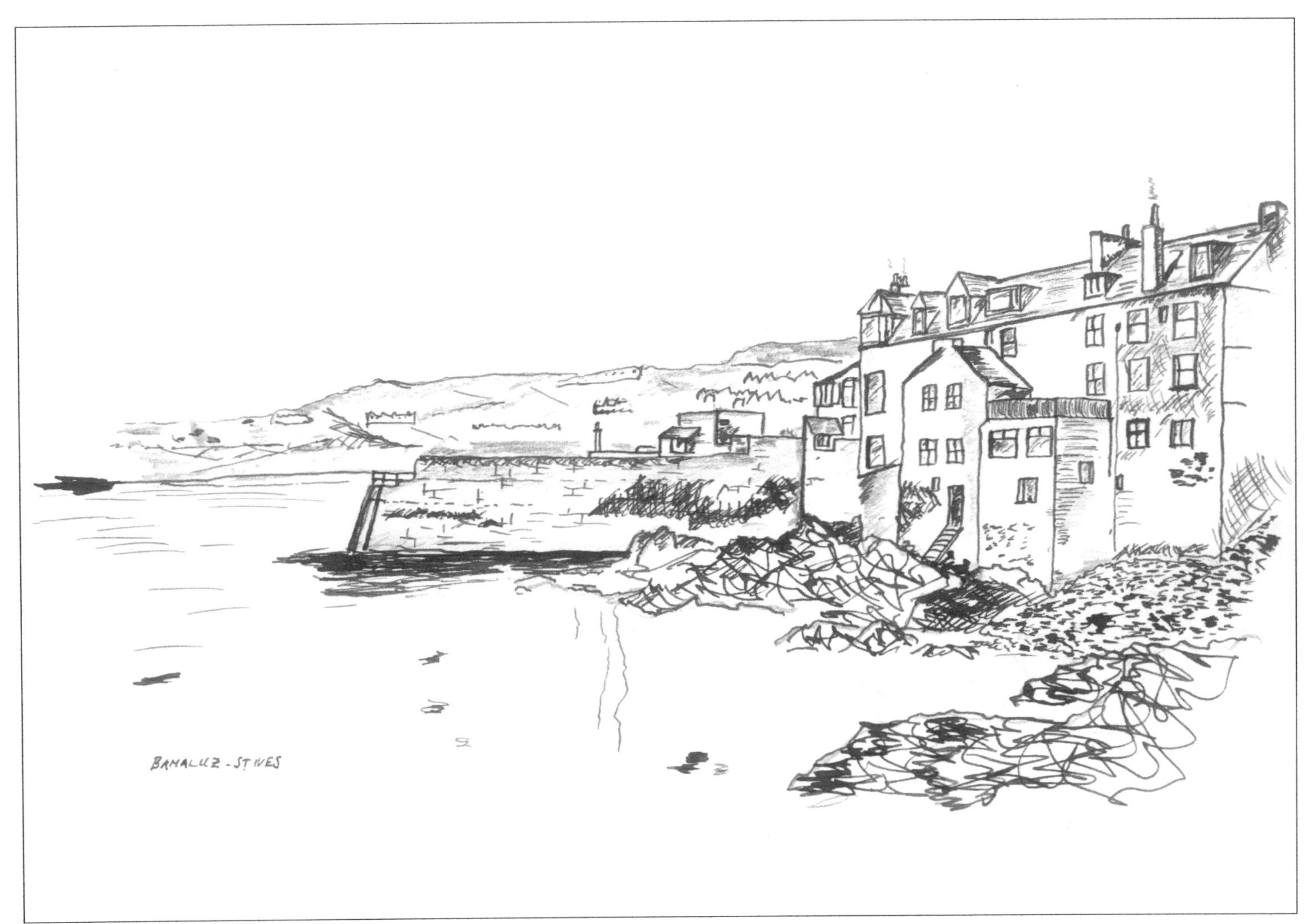
BAMALUZ - ST IVES

PORTHGWIDDEN, ST. IVES

One of St. Ives' smaller beaches, and hidden beneath the island, Porthgwidden is sheltered on the edge of St. Ives Bay and enjoys an uninterrupted view all the way across to the Godrevy Lighthouse.

Its lines of tiered beach huts and a very good cafe and restaurant give it something of an exclusive feel... The beach is small, with quite a large tidal range, but it never seems to get as crowded as its much larger and popular neighbour, Porthmeor - probably because of the latter's more active surf.

In the background is the old coastguard lookout, now manned by volunteers after coastguard operations were centralised over in Falmouth. It is built into the old 1850s Crimean War battery which consisted of three circular gun emplacements and an arsenal, which still has evidence of loopholes for muskets.

The guns were removed at the end of the 19th century, but the stout granite emplacements remain. It's really worth heading up there in almost any weather because the views are breathtaking. Dramatic and tempestuous in a squall and wonderfully clear when it's fine, you can see nearly 40 miles up to Trevose Head when conditions are good.

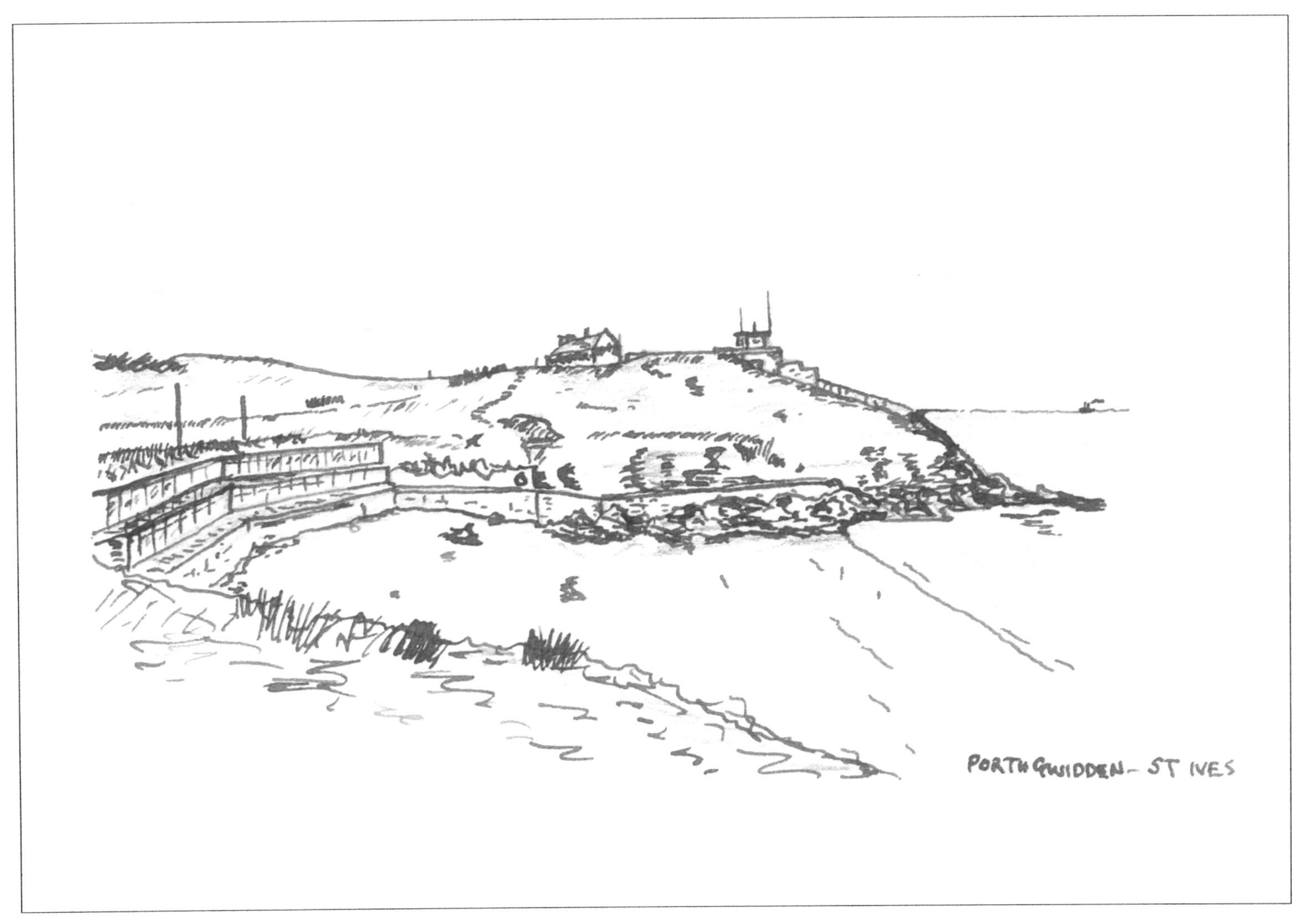

PORTHGWIDDEN - ST IVES

THE ISLAND, ST. IVES

Not an island, but in fact, an isthmus, 'The Island' forms an emerald backdrop to the streets of 'Downalong' and, in many ways, acts as a park for St. Ives. Apart from the tiny 'Trewyn' gardens, there's no open green space in the town.

It's always worth making an effort to walk up to its twin peaks, as the 360-degree views over the town, up and down the coast, and out into the Atlantic are spectacular in any weather!

There's a path that takes you around from the car park in a clockwise direction which skirts above the rocky shoreline and brings you up at the old arsenal and gun battery. It's an invigorating walk - in all but the calmest conditions there's always a persistent breeze that can be exhilarating when the weather becomes more tempestuous.

I'd say it's best avoided when the storms come - you'll get a thorough dousing from the Atlantic if you do! If you are an inveterate storm watcher, wrap up and head up to St. Nicholas's Chapel to get the thrills but not the danger…..

The townward side of the island has a gentle slope which has always been inviting for children to play and roll down. I remember well how this became the main sledging site on those rare occasions when snow penetrated as far south as St. Ives…

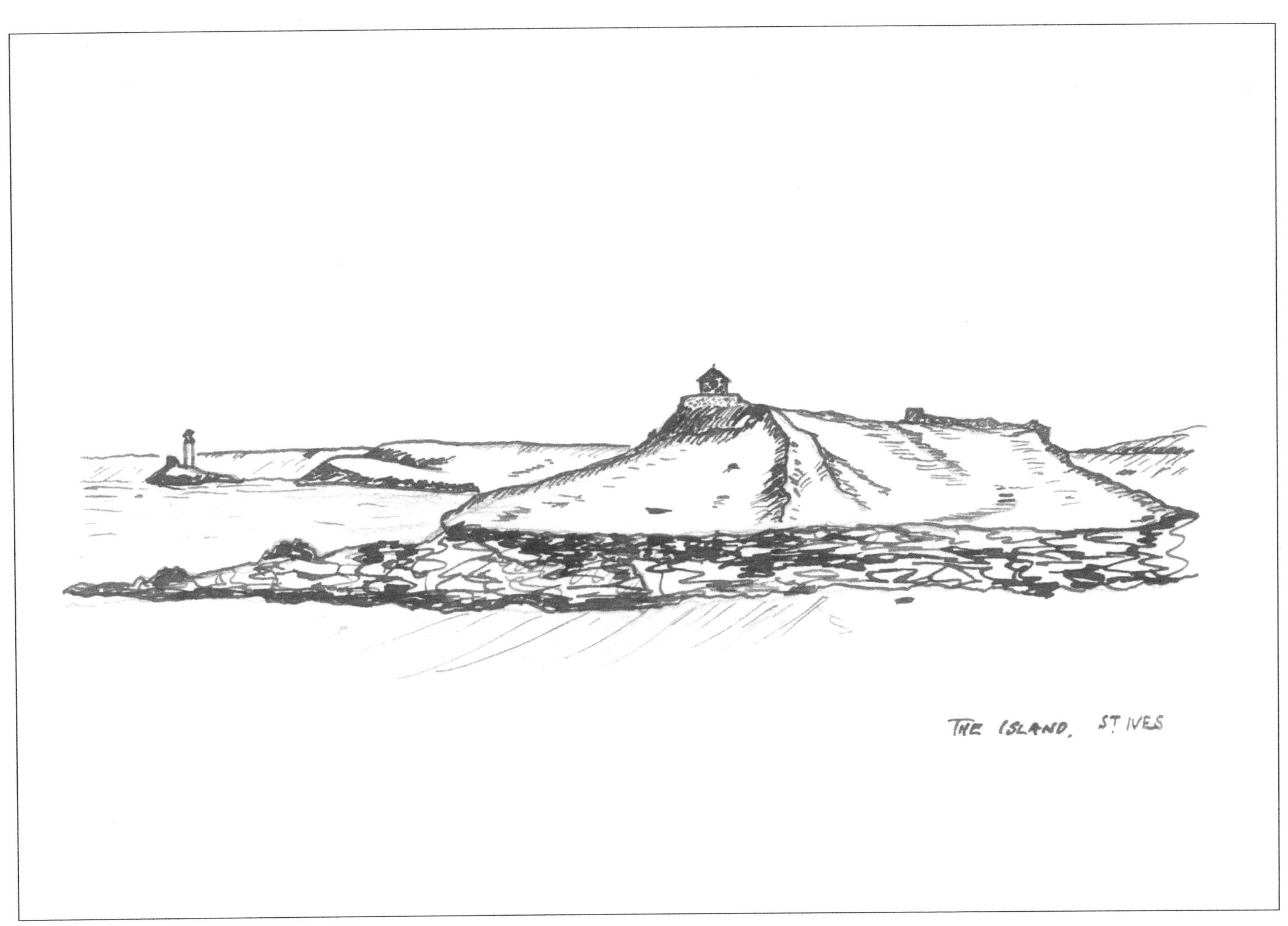

THE ISLAND. ST IVES

ST. NICHOLAS'S CHAPEL, THE ISLAND, ST. IVES

Dedicated to the patron saint of children and sailors, this tiny chapel is no longer used for services but is now becoming increasingly popular for post-wedding blessings.

Though an ancient site of worship, there is no actual record of when the original chapel was built. There is reference to a chapel here before the Parish Church of St. Ia was built in 1425.

For most of the latter half of the 19th century, it was actually owned and used by the War Ministry as a store for the nearby gun battery, but when tensions with France eased, and the battery was decommissioned, the Ministry demolished the former chapel to a huge public outcry in 1904. The current building was built in 1911 and paid for by public subscription.

It's a beautiful spot and has panoramic views across the bay, the town, and the Atlantic. Take something warm when you visit though - there's always a cooling breeze.

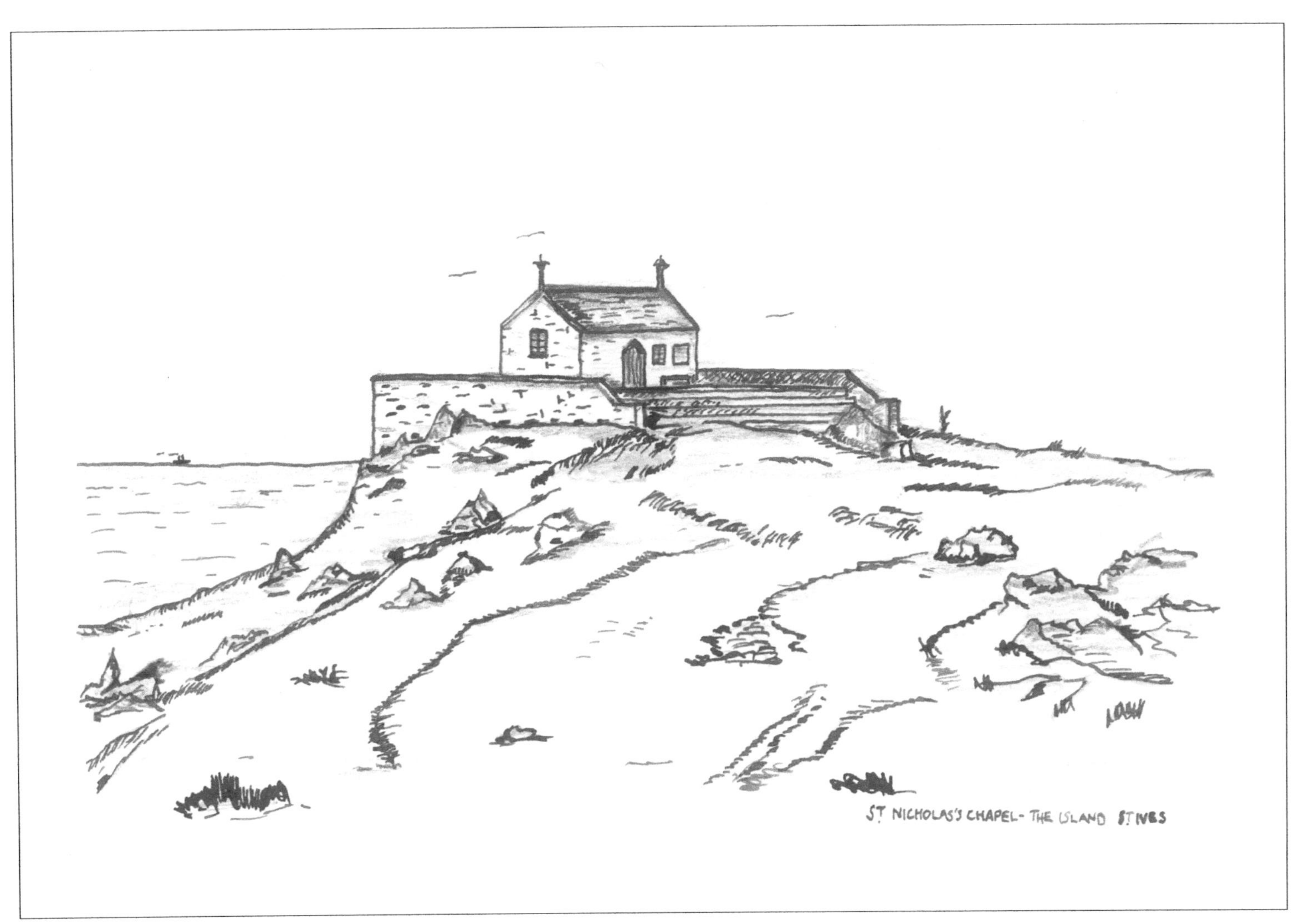

ST NICHOLAS'S CHAPEL- THE ISLAND ST IVES

TATE, ST. IVES

Built on the site of the old gasworks, the architecture of the main gallery of Tate St. Ives actually echoes the old Gasometer that once stood overlooking St. Ives' premier surfing beach - Porthmeor.

An iconic building with more than a few nods to Art Deco influences, it is a fitting venue to celebrate the artists that formed the cutting edge of post-war art and also the newer generation of creatives.

It's very easy to find via Fore Street, The Digey, and Back Road West, and - if you go that way - you'll actually pass the former home of the 'naïve' style painter and mariner Alfred Wallis, who inspired the generation of interwar artists to take a new direction with their work.

Ben Nicholson and Christopher 'Kit' Wood literally stumbled upon Wallis by a chance look through his open cottage doorway as he painted 'for company' after his wife had passed away. Though Whistler and Sickert had hailed the start of the town's artistic life in the 19th and early 20th centuries, it was these two and their championship of Wallis that really put St. Ives on the artistic map.

The aftermath of the Second World War and the arrival of artists like Gabo, Frost, and sculptor Barbara Hepworth, in turn, created the crucible of modern art that St. Ives became....

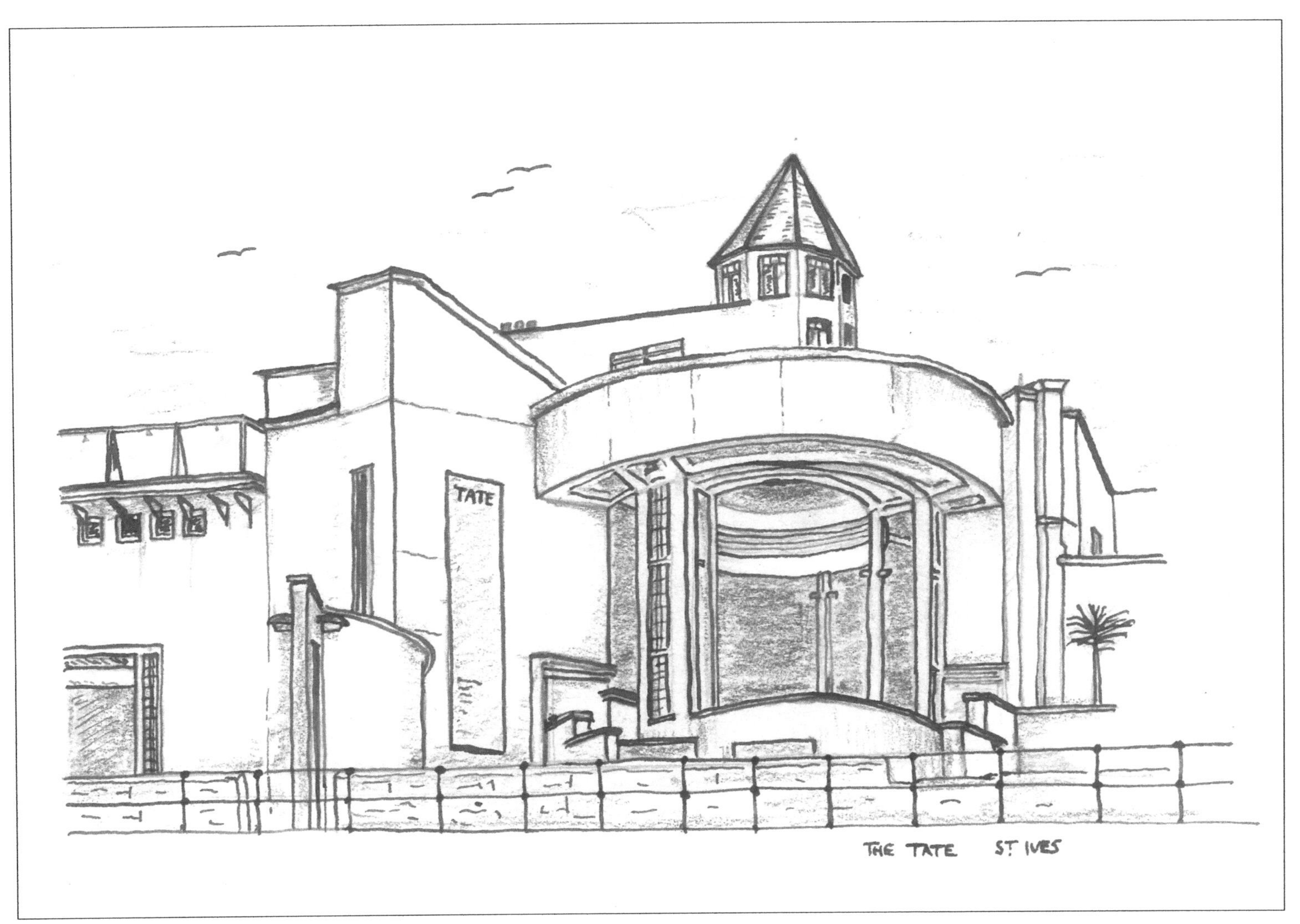

TATE
THE TATE   ST. IVES

MAN'S HEAD, ST. IVES

At the opposite end of Porthmeor Beach from the island is Man's Head. So called because of an oddly perched rock at the top of the headland, which resembles a crusty old chap with a short back and sides.

A little inland from the head is the remains of Carthew Quarry, which for many years was fenced off, and we were forbidden to play there. But, inevitably, we did!

As school friends, we also used to regularly swim by the rocks on Man's Head because it was quieter than Porthmeor Beach during the holidays. One particularly daring game was to jump across a narrow gap in the rocks, with the sea boiling and crashing beneath. It was pretty silly really, because it could easily have been a messy business if you got the jump wrong and then fell into the water below…

Sometimes we'd just jump in anyway and be swept along helplessly to then emerge breathless and exhilarated on the tiny sandy beach at its landward end.

Clambering on the rocks of the headland behind the remains of two demolished World War 2 pillboxes was a frequent pastime in summer or winter, and it was here I took a nasty tumble, got a rearranged nose, and a trip to the local Edward Hain hospital for my trouble!!!

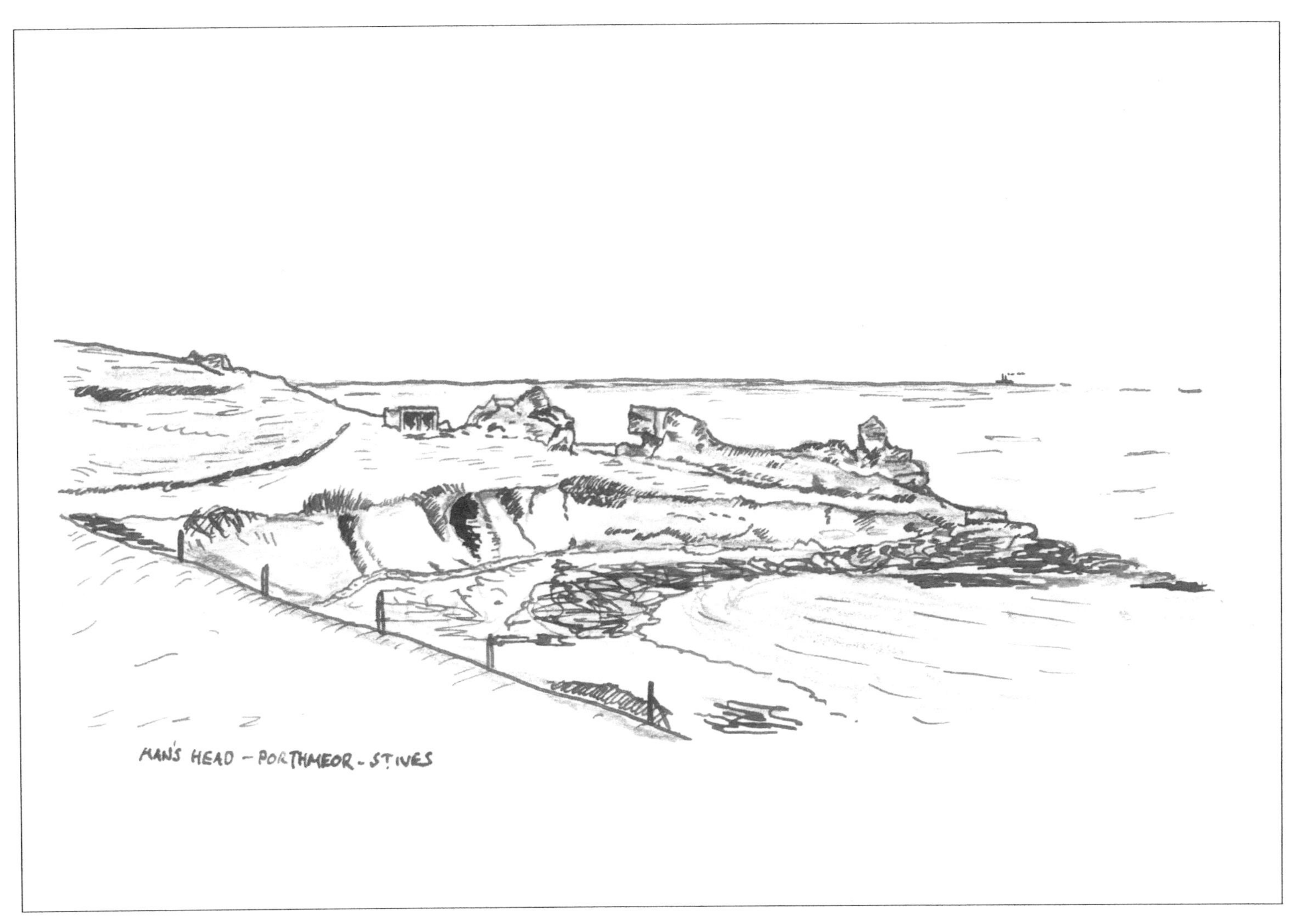

MAN'S HEAD - PORTHMEOR - ST IVES

THE TINNERS ARMS, ZENNOR

If you head out of St. Ives towards Land's End along the B3306, you will enjoy a drive through some of the wildest parts of Cornwall. It's a landscape of ancient monuments forbidding hills and the romance of 'Poldark Country'.

Along the way, you'll pass by 'Eagles Nest', the spectacularly positioned former home of artist Patrick Heron and - after some winding turns - the first settlement you encounter is the small village of Zennor. DH Lawrence lived here for a couple of years before being asked to leave (I think he was suspected of signalling to U boats in the First World War!).

The heart of Zennor consists of St. Senara's Church (13th century) and this delightful pub: The Tinners Arms.
Local legend has it that if you run three times anti-clockwise around the outside of the Church, you'll disappear because the Devil will cart you off. Nothing is mentioned about running the other way, but I find the idea of an early arrival in 'The other place' not such an appealing alternative either!!

What is much more enticing - and far less strenuous - is what's on offer at 'The Tinners'. I have very fond memories of this being a regular evening jaunt for all of us with close family friends Uncle Reg, Sheila, and their sons Simon and Paul - who were the same sort of age as my brother and me.

We weren't allowed in the pub, so the four boys would have a soft drink in the garden and then run a short way down the lane to play in the clear stream and see if there were fish to be caught. Warm summer evenings bathed in a copper sunset - Halcyon Days….

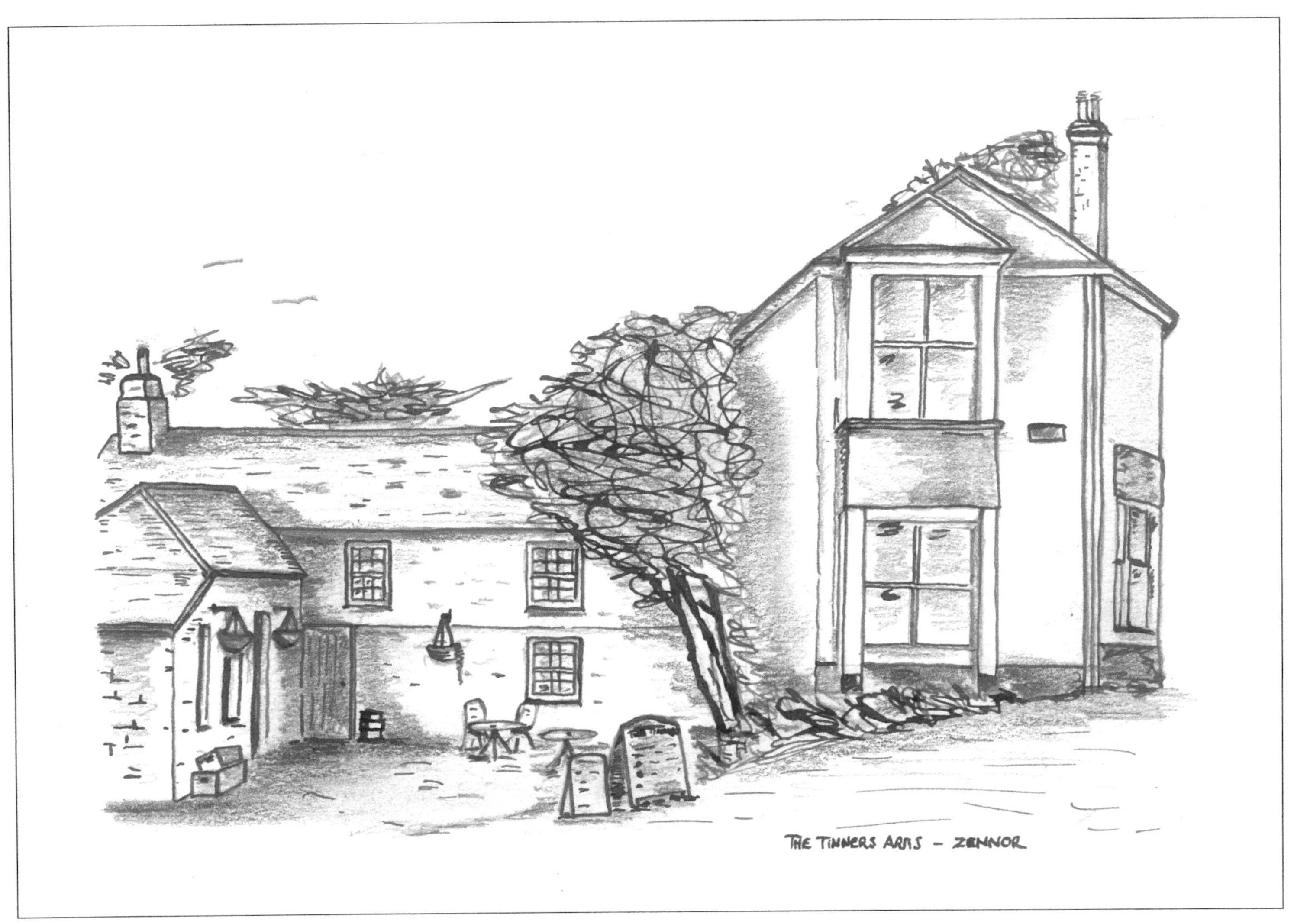

THE TINNERS ARMS - ZENNOR

BOTALLACK MINE

The definitive image of Cornwall. Of the rugged cliffs, the sea, and crumbling tin mines.

The Cornish landscape is peppered with the relics of this once ubiquitous industry, which began in the Bronze Age and declined from the mid-19th century until the last mine closed in 1998.

There were also copper, lead, and - in places - arsenic mines. Even within the towns themselves, the names of former mines reveal themselves: Wheal Dream and Pedn Olva mines were on the skirts of the harbour of St. Ives, and the former Wheal Ayr was a hundred yards from where we lived…

Botallack Mine was part of a huge proliferation of workings around the St. Just and Pendeen areas, of which only the Geevor Tin Mine survives as a museum. Many of its workings lie out under the sea and there is still tin to be mined from them, though it is no longer economically viable to do so.

Designated a World Heritage Site, its famous engine houses, clinging to the cliffs, are a dramatic monument to an industry that once provided employment to tens of thousands and supplied all of the UK's tin.

"The winding engines used to sing,
A melody to Cornish tin,
And Geevor lads they all would grin,
At pay day on a Friday."

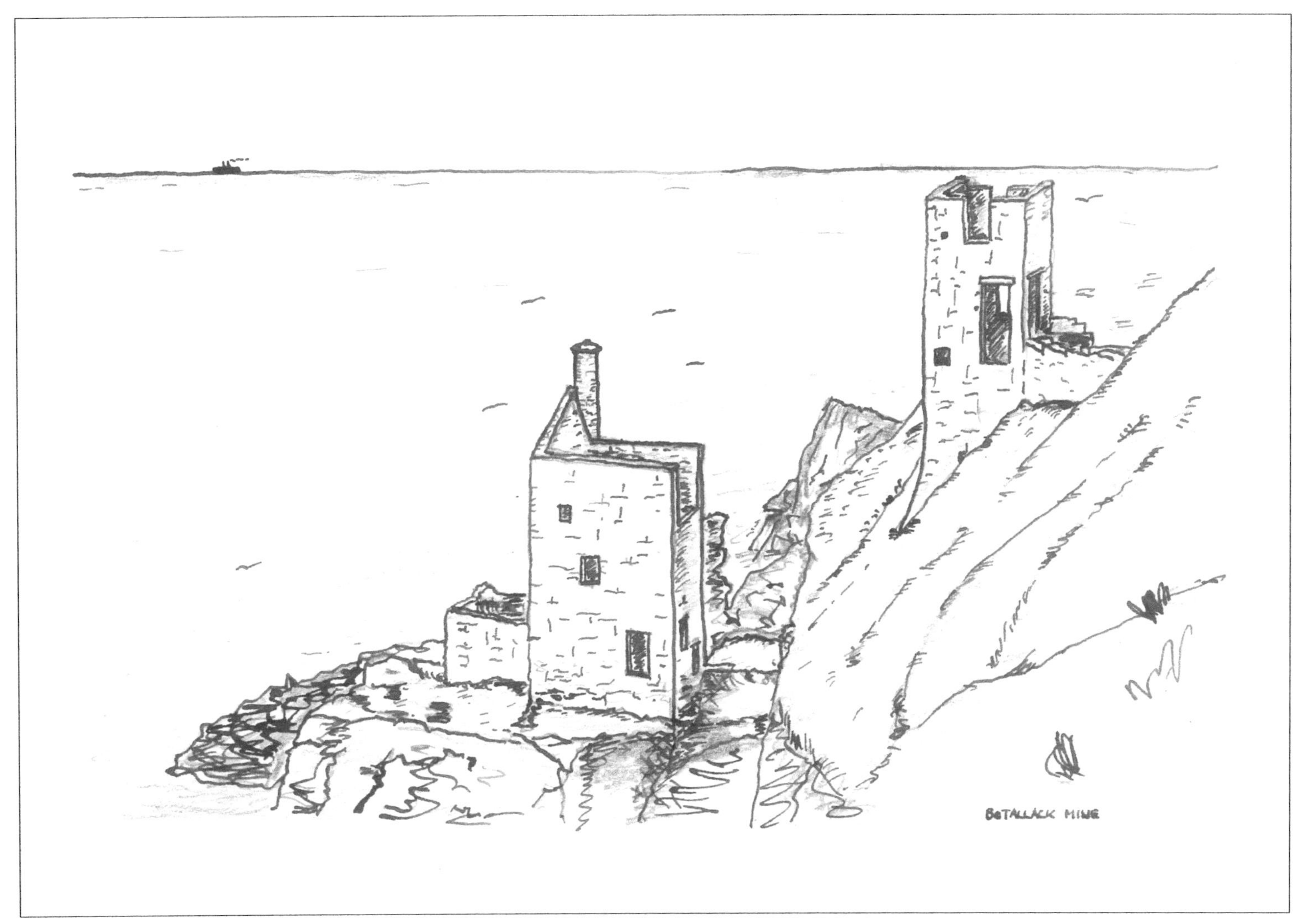
BOTALLACK MINE

CAPE CORNWALL, ST. JUST

The headland of Cape Cornwall near St. Just is a mere four miles from Land's End and, until the 19th century ordnance survey, was actually believed to be Land's End itself.

For many years the Cape was private land, but in the 1980s, it was purchased by HJ Heinz (of baked beans fame!) and given to the National Trust. A case of Beanz meanz a gift to the nation, I suppose!!!

At the foot of the landward end of the headland are the remains of yet another tin mine whose chimney right at the top of the Cape was left standing as an aid to navigation. Just in front of this is the old coastguard lookout, which, in its discrete and desolate solitude, looks out towards the Brisons Rocks a mile off.

The Brisons were always a favoured spot for my father's all-day fishing voyages from St. Ives and later Hayle when he moved his boat there. From the Brisons he would return with pollock and seabass for my mother to fillet and then freeze, which would then be served periodically for evening meals… even though despite being an avid fisherman, my father was not overly keen on eating fish!!!

It all looks benign on a breezy summer's day, but it can be ferocious when the weather turns. Walking up to the summit by the chimney is a bracing experience and needs to be carefully considered in a storm - you can easily be blown off your feet!

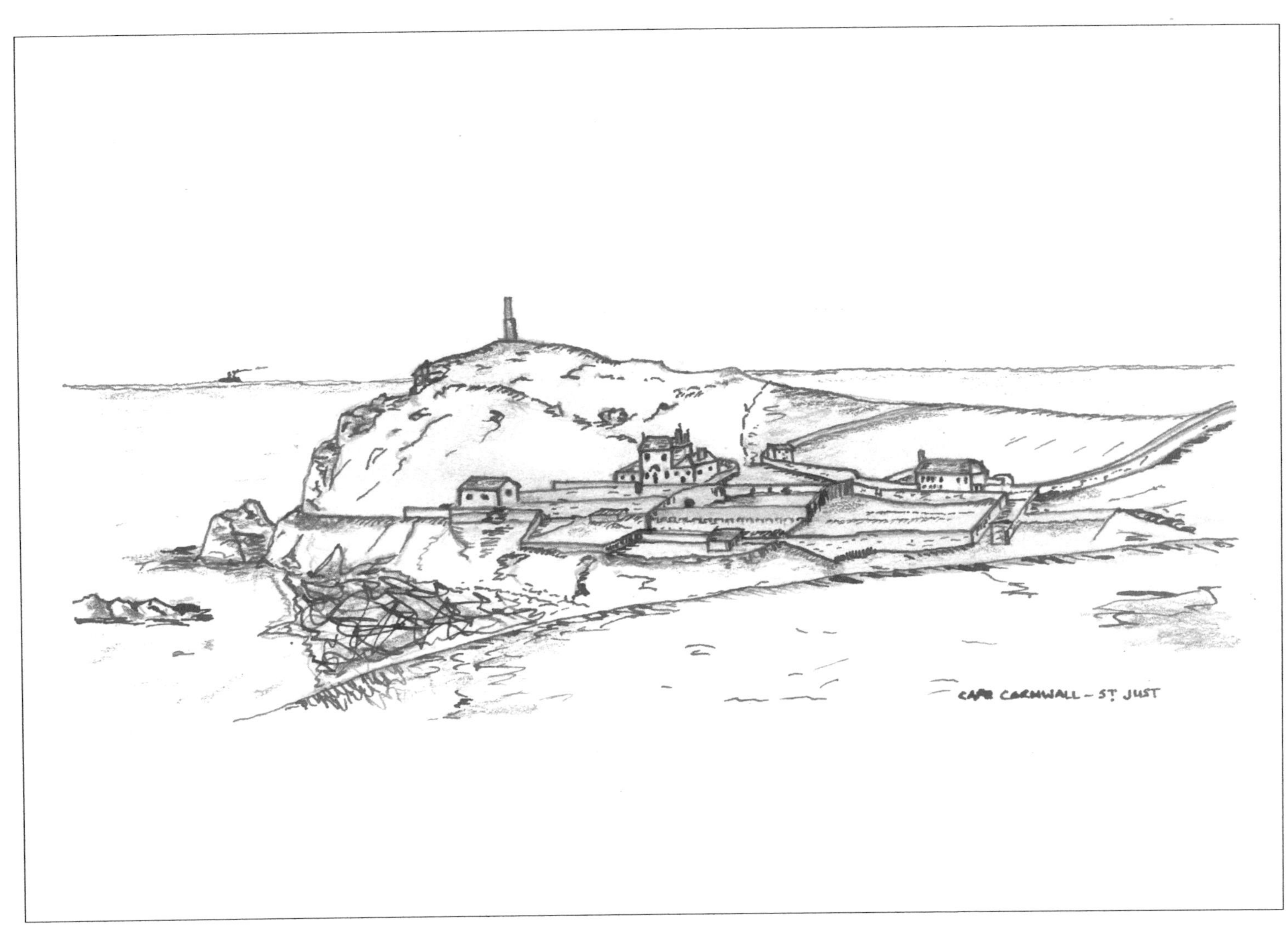
CAPE CORNWALL - ST JUST

LAND'S END

The furthest westerly point in mainland England. An iconic spot that marks the beginning and end of many a pilgrimage, fundraiser or marathon journey of discovery.

The signpost marking the spot gives an indication of how far away New York or São Paulo are, and the combination of this, and the sight of the Atlantic stretching away, gives one the sobering realisation that perhaps the world isn't quite as small as some would have us believe.

On a clear and sunny day, you can see two lighthouses: the closest is Longships; then a little further, the distant speck of Wolf Rock. Bishop Rock Lighthouse is four miles west of the Isles of Scilly, and just out of sight. The outline of the Isles of Scilly can also be made out. According to legend, the Kingdom of Lionesse lies sunken between here and the islands.

In the summer months, there is an open-topped bus service from St. Ives via Land's End to Penzance that follows the coast road through Zennor and St. Just. It is the best way to see this stunning part of the world if the weather is fine. The sun and breeze can be deceptive, however, and oft is the time when someone is caught out and returns to the Malakoff in St. Ives looking rather tomato-like!!!

"We'd searched the seven stones all around,
But not a sign nor shoal we found,
Round Island's light is now in sight,
But Scillies are a barren ground."

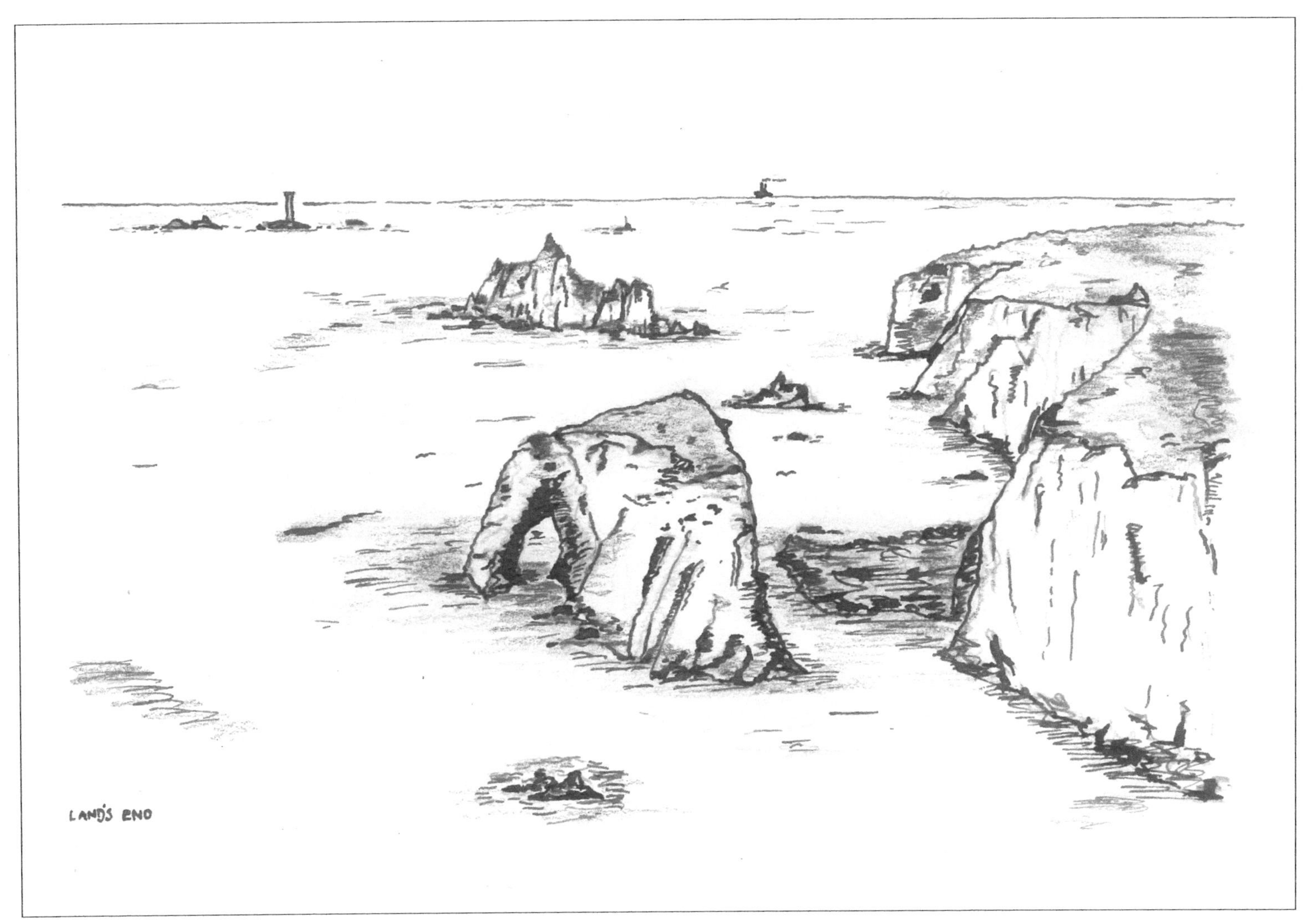

LAND'S END

LONGSHIPS LIGHTHOUSE, LAND'S END

Built in 1875, Longships Lighthouse was the third such to occupy the island one and a quarter miles off the treacherous coast of Land's End where 130 shipwrecks have been recorded.

Equipped with the most advanced technology of the time, it was still nearly demolished when the steamer SS Bluejacket ran onto the rock on a clear night in 1904!

The keepers - two at a time in shifts - were housed with their families in a purpose-built terrace in Sennen, which faces towards the lighthouse. So the poor devils couldn't escape the place even when they weren't on duty!

It's a wild spot, and it was always known to be problematic to supply in the winter or in any kind of swell. On one occasion in the 1890s, the keepers ran short of tobacco and were reduced to smoking a brew of dried hops and coffee - so it must have come as a relief when the helipad was installed in 1974.

The light was only manned for another fourteen years before it was automated in 1988, and since 1996 it has been remotely monitored by Trinity House from Harwich…

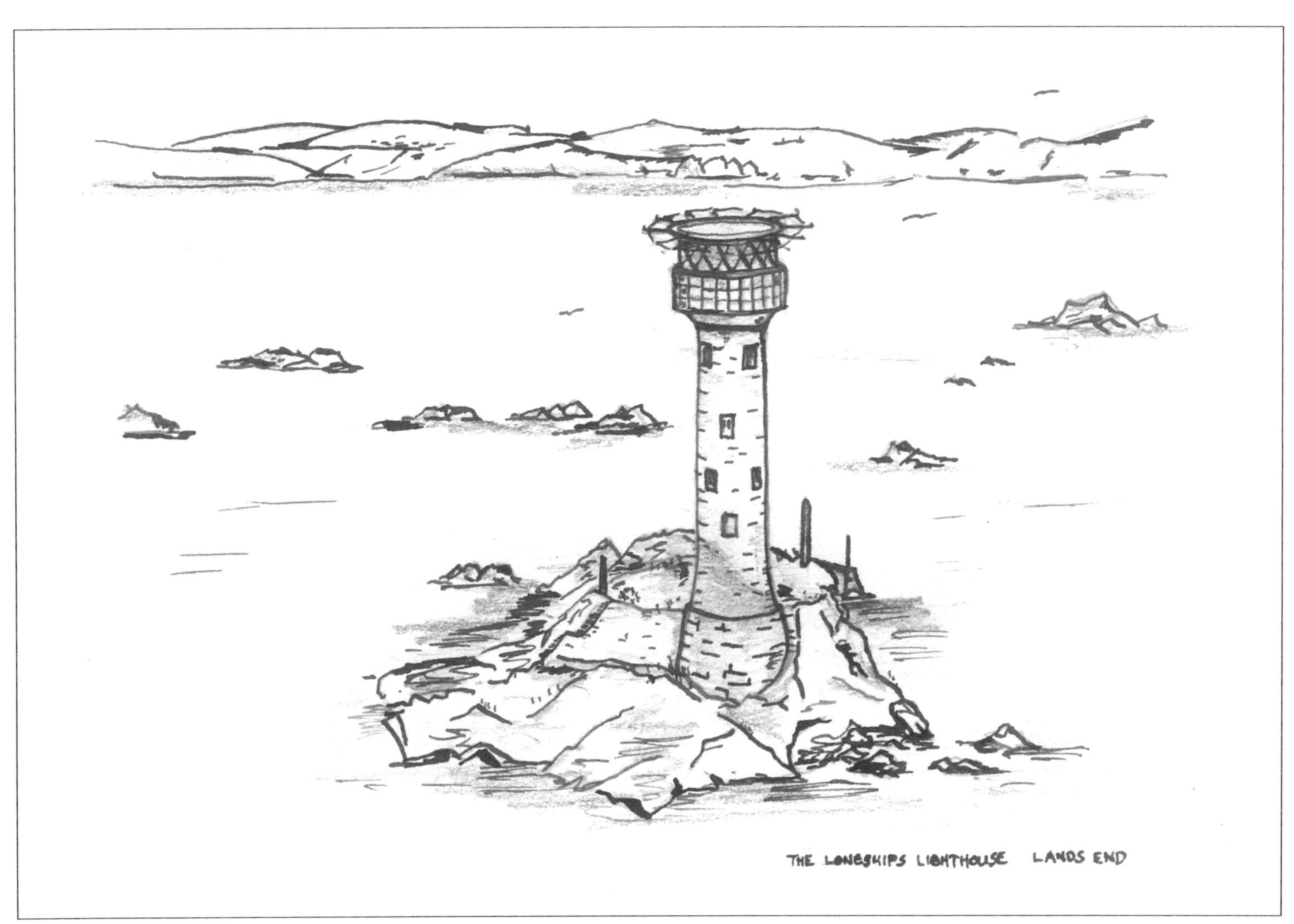

THE LONGSHIPS LIGHTHOUSE   LANDS END

THE MINACK THEATRE, PORTHCURNO

Both surreal and magical, The Minack must be the most dramatic setting for any theatre (the name in Cornish means Rocky Place!).

Built almost exclusively with hand tools, the theatre was carved out of the rocky cliff as the life's work of local artist Rowena Cade, from the mid-1930s to the early 1980s.

A classic case of 'If you build it, they will come', the Minack is now a successful theatre that attracts just over a quarter of a million visitors a year, and its productions gain even greater gravitas from the carved granite amphitheater and the sounds of the sea. Watching Shakespeare on a balmy summer's evening as the sun sets is an unforgettable experience and not one to forego.

It's wise to be prepared however, because those granite seats can tax even the most upholstered of rear-ends in performances of a few hours, and once the sun dips, it can get a little chilly even at the warmest of times.

I can remember watching the St. Ives band play here before I began learning to play. The evening was perfect apart from the occasional gust of a breeze. Then disaster struck with a sudden violent blast, and half the music took flight into the sea......that was the end of that piece!!!

Nearby is the deeply shelved sandy beach and the hamlet of Porthcurno. It's hard to grasp that here all the transatlantic and worldwide communication cables run up into an almost unnoticeable concrete shed!!!

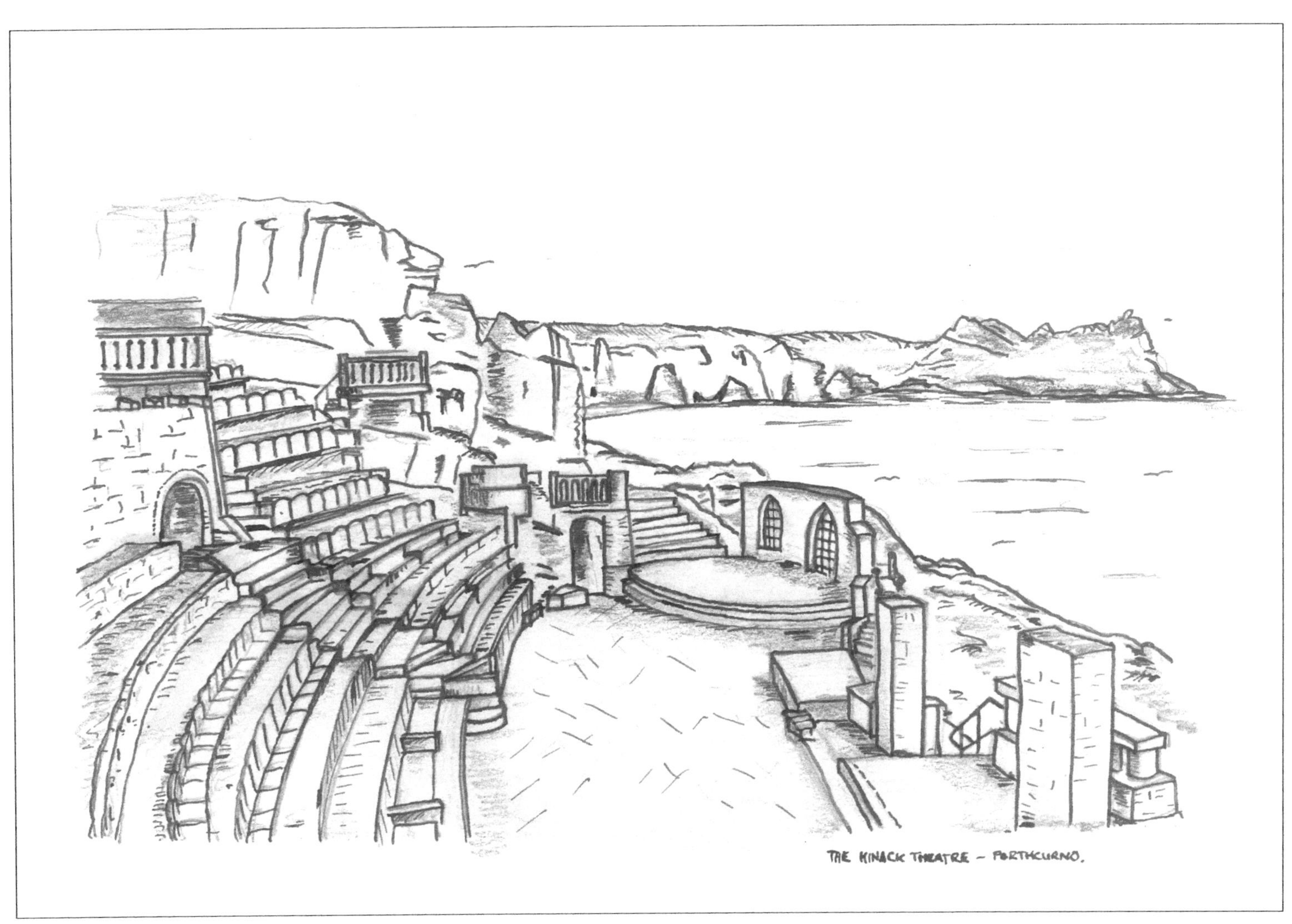

THE MINACK THEATRE - PORTHCURNO.

LAMORNA COVE

"Twas down in Albert Square,
I never shall forget,
Her eyes they shone like diamonds,
And the evening it was wet, wet, wet,
And her hair hung down in curls,
She was a charming rover,
And we rode all night,
Through the pale moonlight,
Away down to Lamorrrnaaaa!!!!"

No Cornish male voice choir concert is complete without this, the most quintessential of Penwith local songs. Lamorna is just along the coast between Mousehole and Porthcurno and is roughly four miles from Penzance - though it feels far more remote than this short distance might suggest!

The small hamlet was a haven for Post-Impressionist artists and those of the Newlyn School from the early part of the 20th century, and many artists and potters continue to live in the vicinity to this day. Even the thriller writer John le Carré lived nearby!

The short harbour wall was constructed to transport the granite that was quarried above the cove to nearby Penzance in the 18th and early 19th centuries. Even now, the remains of that activity can be seen in the huge granite boulders strewn on the hillsides…. The cove is, surprisingly, privately owned and this might go some way to explaining why it has remained undeveloped and unspoiled in an era where everything has marketable value. This lack of development does still attract commercial interest because it is used for period drama filming on occasion.

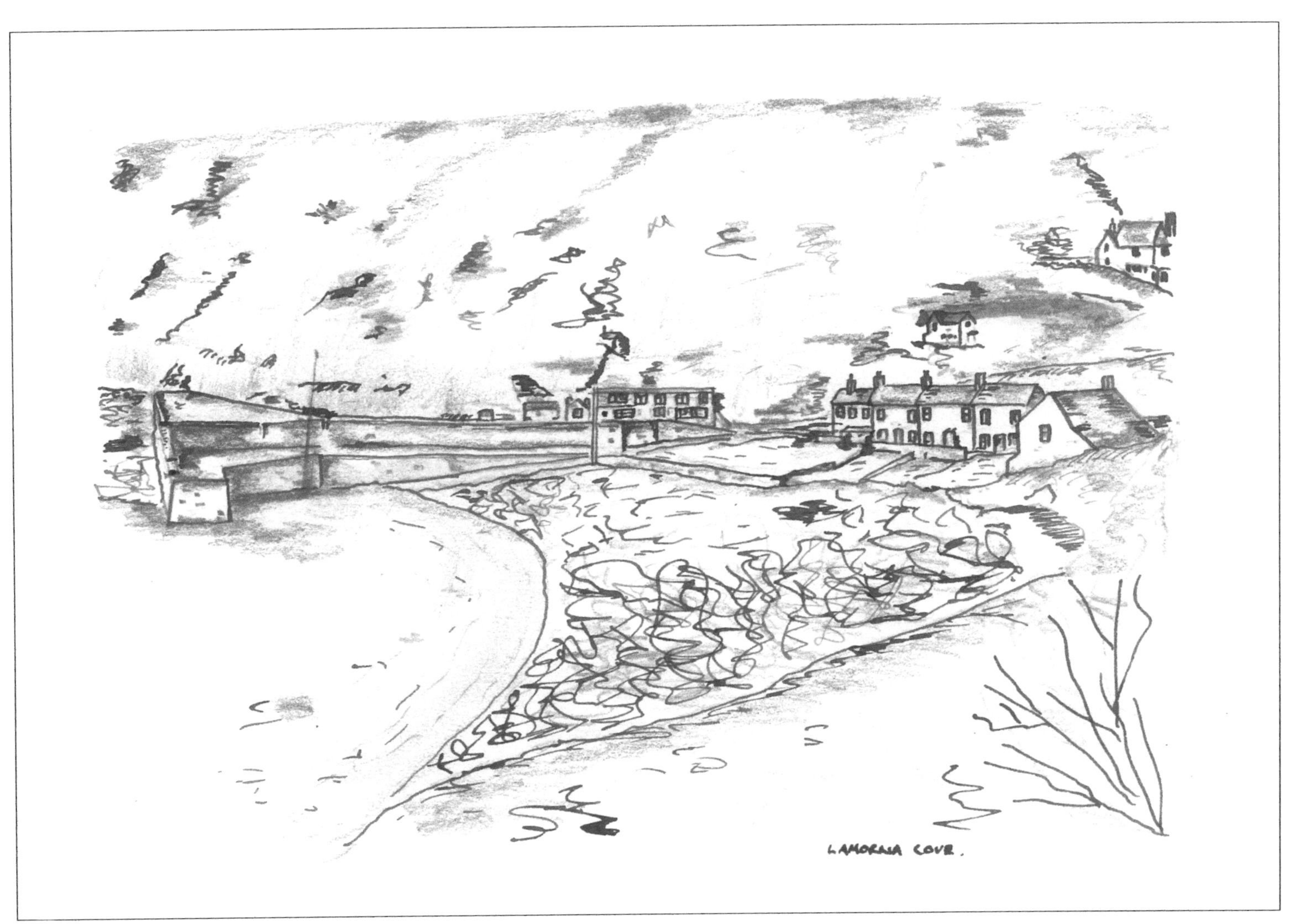

LAMORNA COVE.

MOUSEHOLE HARBOUR

Picture-perfect 'Mouzel' is the mind's eye version of what a Cornish fishing village should be. With its embracing arms of granite harbour walls and its narrow streets curling up and away in a huddle of jostling cottages, it's hard to imagine anywhere more perfect.

I remember it as an isolated community - the road from Newlyn hugs the coastline to Mousehole only - you can't really go through it to get anywhere. Even the bus has to turn around on the edge of the village because it can't negotiate the narrow streets.

I suppose as a result, it made for a tight-knit community with its own ways, traditions, and even dishes. Stargazy Pie, with mackerel heads poking up through the mashed potato crust, is one of the most memorable!

Though no longer a 'working' fishing port, many of the locals worked the boats out of Newlyn and the local lifeboat. A few worked in the Penlee Quarry around the headland too.

I recall playing in the St. Ives Band for the annual blessing of the Penlee Lifeboat on the quay on balmy summer evenings with the Mousehole Male Voice Choir, and the community gathered about….

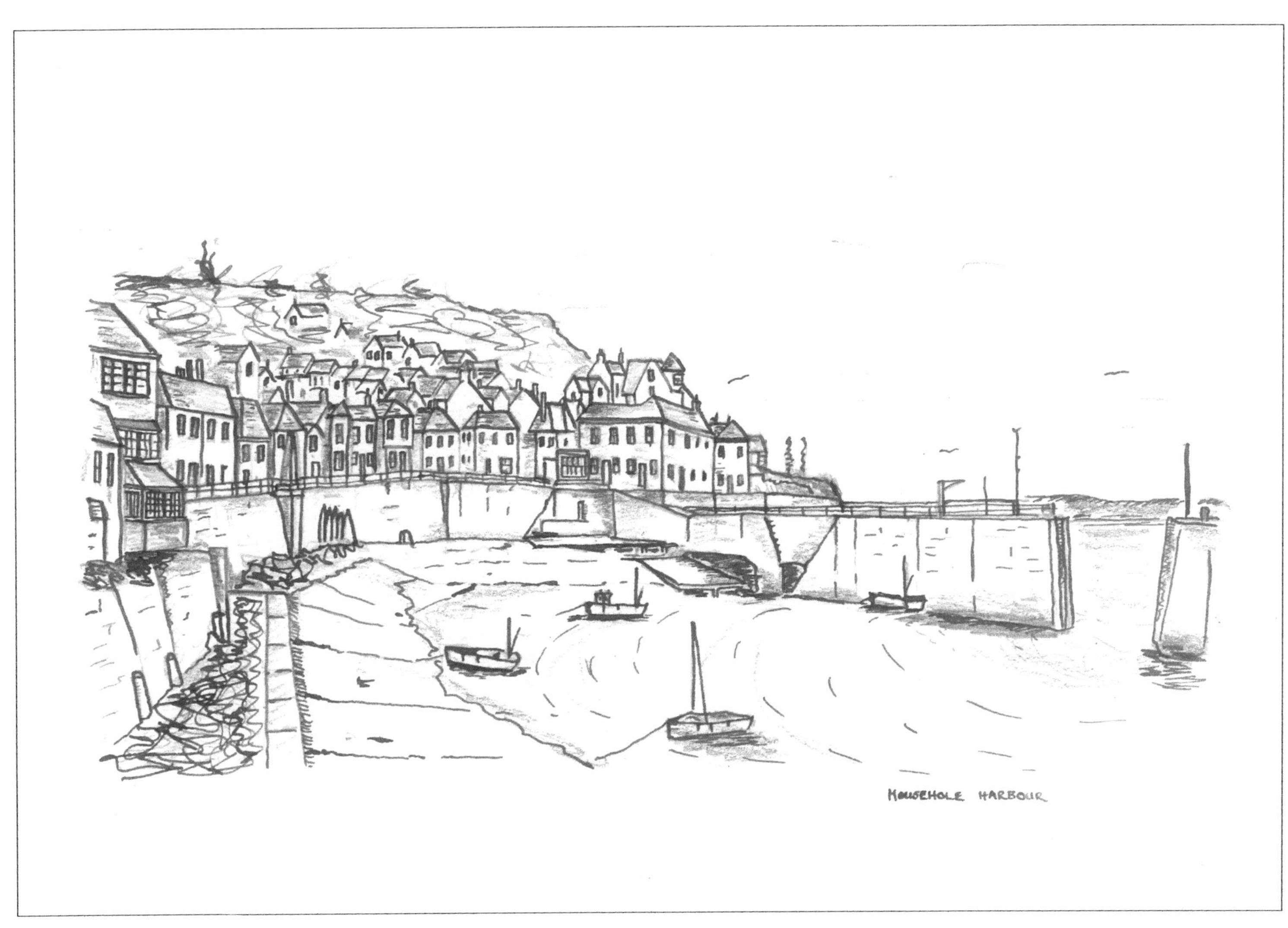

MOUSEHOLE HARBOUR

PENLEE LIFEBOAT, MOUSEHOLE

The current Penlee Lifeboat is based in Newlyn Harbour and has been there since 1981. However, between Mousehole and Newlyn, just below the road level and clinging to the rocks, is the now decommissioned Lifeboat Station on Penlee Point.

It is now an RNLI museum and memorial to the crew of the last lifeboat stationed here - the Solomon Browne - lost with its entire crew on 19th December 1981.

The lifeboat was lost rescuing the crew from the stricken coaster Union Star - the battered and rusty remains of which are still visible a little way up the coast towards Lamorna.

The recording of the Royal Navy rescue helicopter pilot conversing with the Coxswain, who calmly said "We've got four off" whilst in the most appalling of hurricane conditions, and then the terrible silence after all contact was lost, remains one of the most hair-raising things I have ever heard.

I used to play in the St. Ives Band at the 'Blessing of the Lifeboat' service every year, and I remember the lifeboat, its crew, and the shock of that tragedy very well…

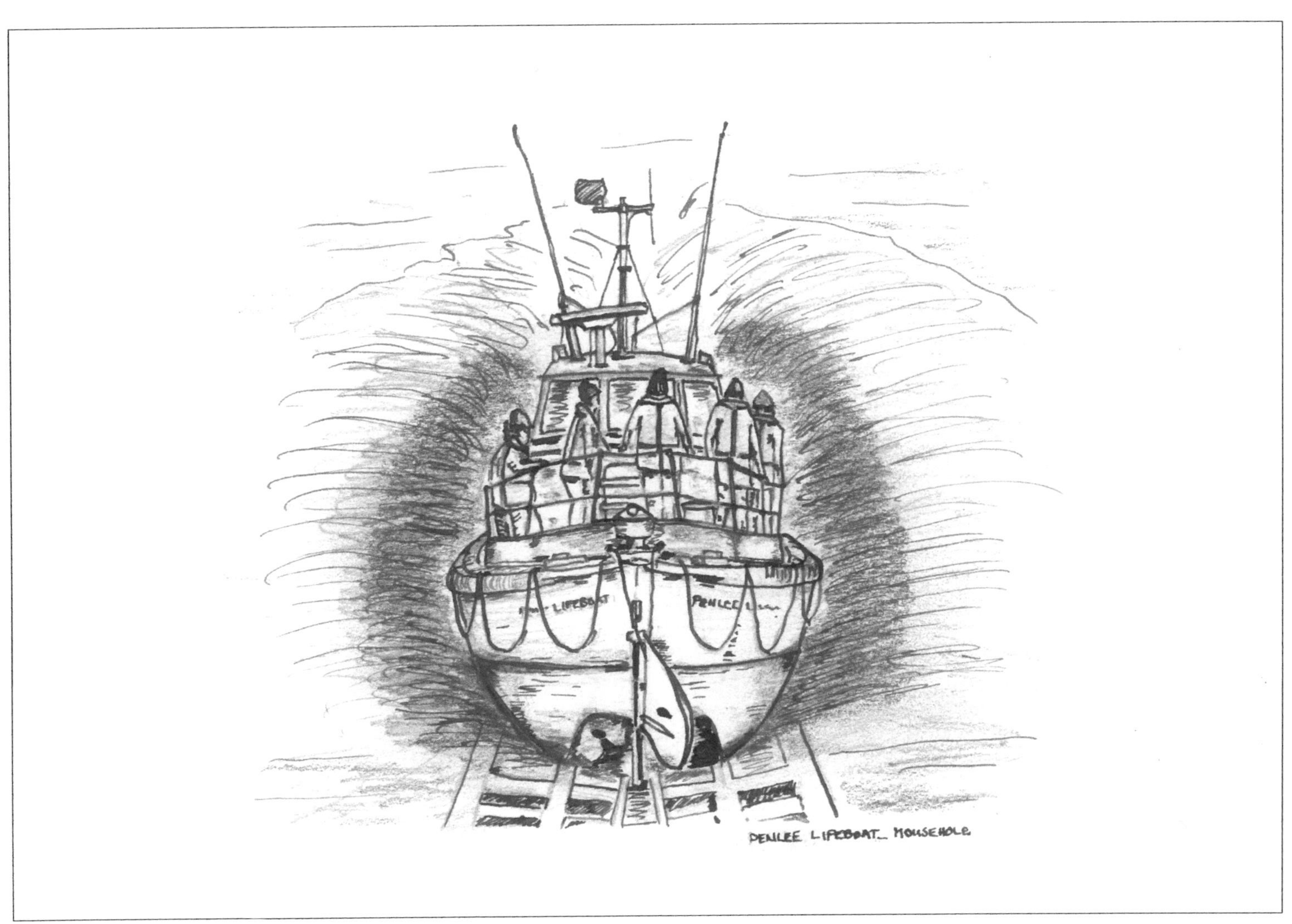

PENLEE LIFEBOAT - MOUSEHOLE

REPAIRS, NEWLYN HARBOUR

Newlyn is the major fishing port in Cornwall and retains the strong sense and tang of a working harbour. The main road through the town takes you through to Mousehole in one direction and to nearby Penzance in the other.

Where the road turns and climbs above the old medieval harbour, one gets a good impression of the modern harbour's size and the extent of the fishing fleet, which always resembles a tangled riot of masts, derricks, and stays.

Here too, is the slipway where even the largest trawler can be hauled out of the water for essential maintenance or inspection. This always makes for an arresting sight exposing, as it does, a vessel out of its natural setting afloat.

On the outer harbour wall next to the red and white lighthouse is an unprepossessing hut which, despite its appearance, is of global significance. This - believe it or not - is the Newlyn Tidal Observatory, which is the home of mean sea level, from which all height measurements in mainland Britain begin.

I can remember wandering along the main quay with my father as a very small boy and feeling the threat of the huge, battered, and rusty trawlers. The treacherous mooring lines and the oily water sluicing beneath an atmosphere heavy with the aroma of diesel, hot metal, brine, and fish….

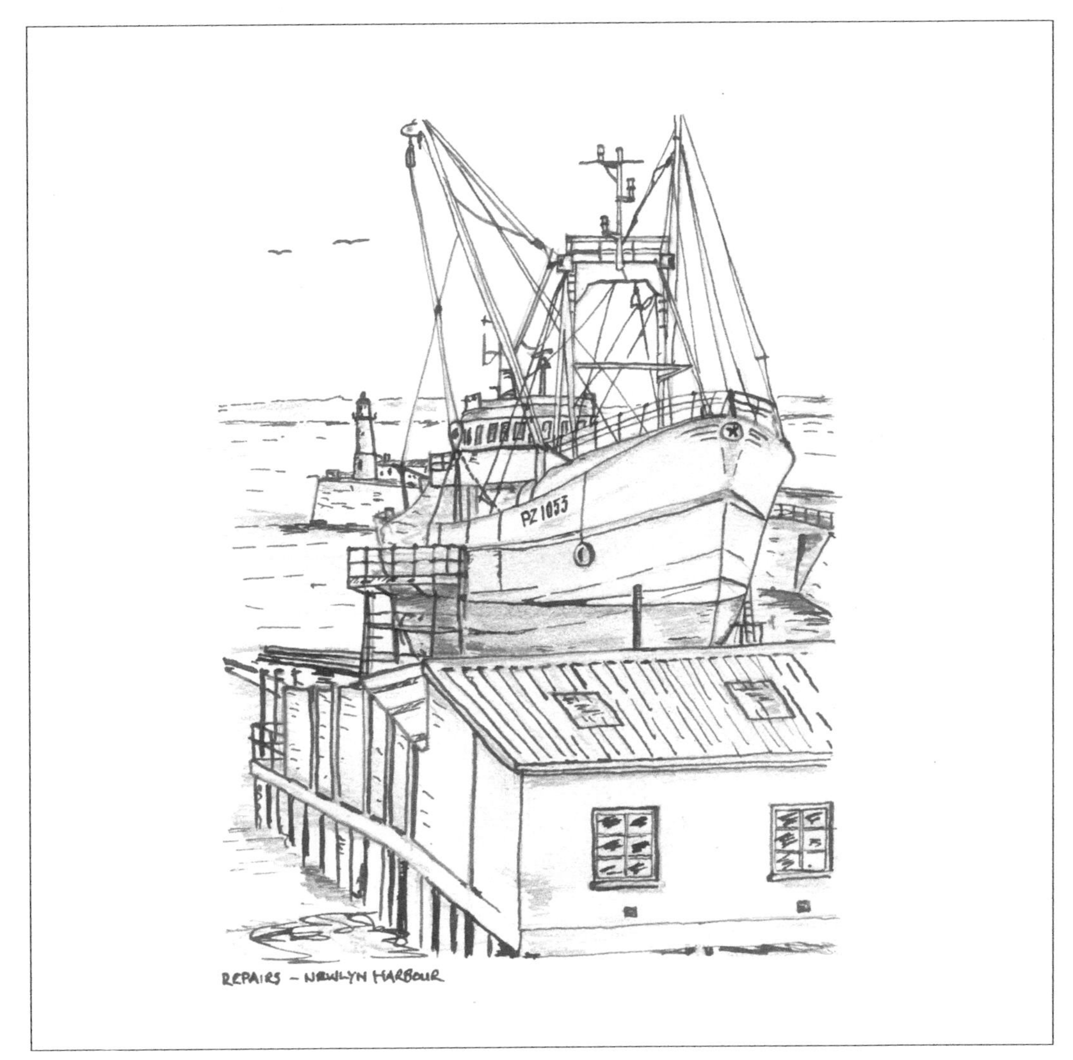

REPAIRS - NEWLYN HARBOUR

SAFELY BACK, NEWLYN HARBOUR

Fishing was one of the staple industries in Cornwall for hundreds of years. The picturesque charms of harbours like St. Ives, Porthleven, Mousehole and Mevagissey, or the quaint sights of Mullion, Cadgwith and Polzeath are now a far cry from the teeming and stinking centres where whole families toiled in near poverty and scratched a hard living from the sea.

It was an exhausting and perilous life, with long exposure to the elements and the potential dangers of shipboard accidents, which resulted in many an early departure for the next world. In fact, even into the early 20th century, to be over 40 years of age as a fisherman was considered to be old. It was no better for those on land either, with the women and children working long hours to process fish, and mend nets and gear before the next trip.

Now in an age of diesel power, hydraulics, fish finders, GPS and radar, it's easy to believe that fishing is safe. It isn't. True - the level of sheer physical hardship is much reduced, but many of the perils and hazards remain. Though much rarer than it was, it's not unheard of to hear of a boat failing to returning in poor weather or of a lifeboat summoned to help a trawler in distress… In a modern age, where commercial fishing is concentrated in a few ports nationally, the population is remote from both its food and how it is harvested, but to see the boats come and go, particularly in the early morning, is a thought-provoking sight.

"From Newlyn town we used to sail,
Through rain and mist and lashing gale,
The mackerel shoals we'd hope to find,
And soon we'd left Land's End behind."

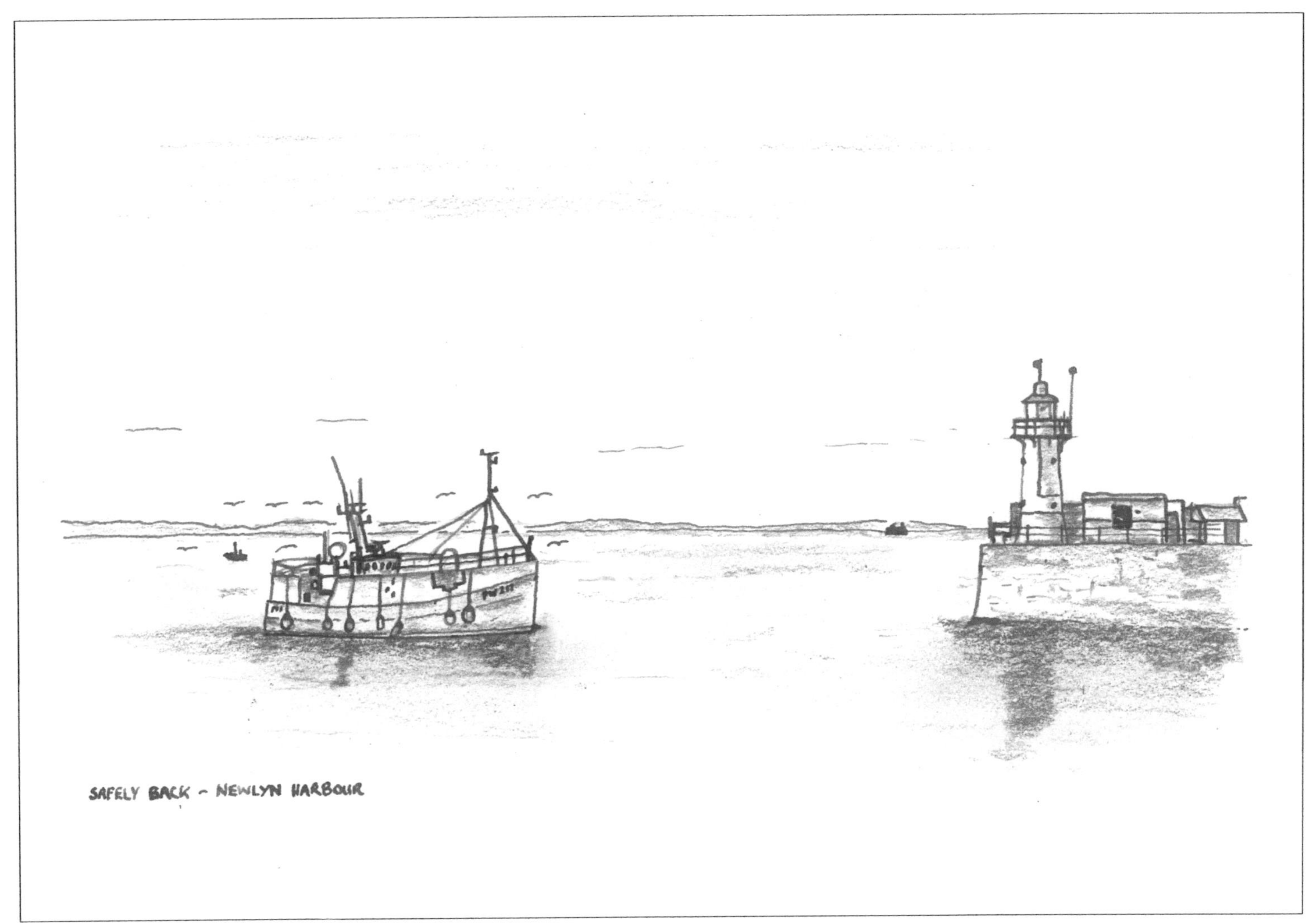

SAFELY BACK - NEWLYN HARBOUR

MARKET JEW STREET, PENZANCE

The street has nothing to do with Jewish people, but, in fact, is a corruption of the Cornish 'Marghas d'Yow' - which literally translates as 'Thursday Market'.

Marghas d'Yow is also the old name for nearby Marazion so there's also an argument for calling it 'Marazion Street'!

At its head, this main thoroughfare of Penzance is dominated by the imposing classical, ionic columned facade of the 1838 granite Market building - which is now largely occupied by the Lloyds Bank.

In front stands a marble statue of Penzance's probably most famous son, Sir Humphrey Davy. Davy is best remembered for his pioneering miners' safety lamp which saved thousands of lives by reducing underground gas explosions. But what many don't realise is that he was a hugely influential chemist who discovered several chemical elements and made vital contributions to science. Had he been born later, he would undoubtedly have been a Nobel Prize winner.

That doesn't spare the noble lord the indignity of regularly being dressed up in drag, or sporting a fetching traffic cone at a jaunty angle after Christmas parties - but such is the fate of public statues, I suppose. I doubt it's personal....

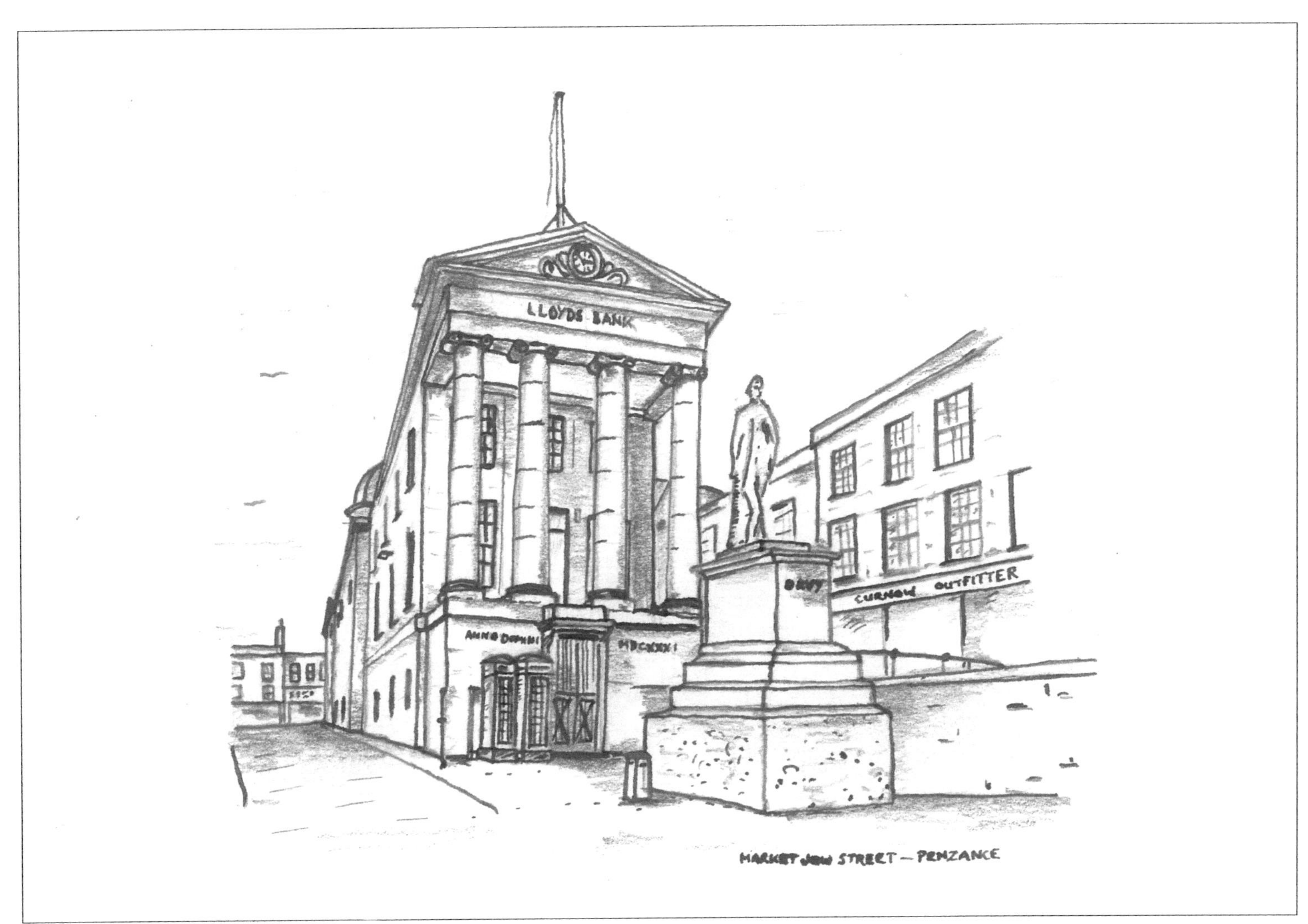

MARKET JEW STREET — PENZANCE

THE 'SCILLONIAN', PENZANCE HARBOUR

The Scillonian III is the most recent bearer of the name for the regular ferry service from Penzance to Hugh Town, St. Mary's on the Isles of Scilly. Launched in 1977, she is now a venerable craft. In all but the roughest weather, she has shuttled to and fro, and is the principal means of supply and transportation for the islands. She is something of a local institution.

For a while, there was a rival British Airways helicopter service from nearby Eastern Green, but this was discontinued when BA decided to axe the service. There was a huge outcry when it was announced! I believe a private service has been reinstated in more recent times…

To enable her to ground at low tide in St. Mary's, the Scillonian is flat-bottomed rather than keeled. This, though practical from that standpoint, does make her a lively ship in a swell - and rare will be the time that there isn't a sea running where the currents meet at Land's End!

Thus, good sea legs and a strong stomach are huge advantages when making the crossing! I vividly recall a whole class from St. Ives School hanging over the railings, green and helpless, on a school trip one Easter!!

It's worth the potential discomfort, as there are few finer places on earth than these islands. A subtropical paradise a mere 20 miles from the mainland…

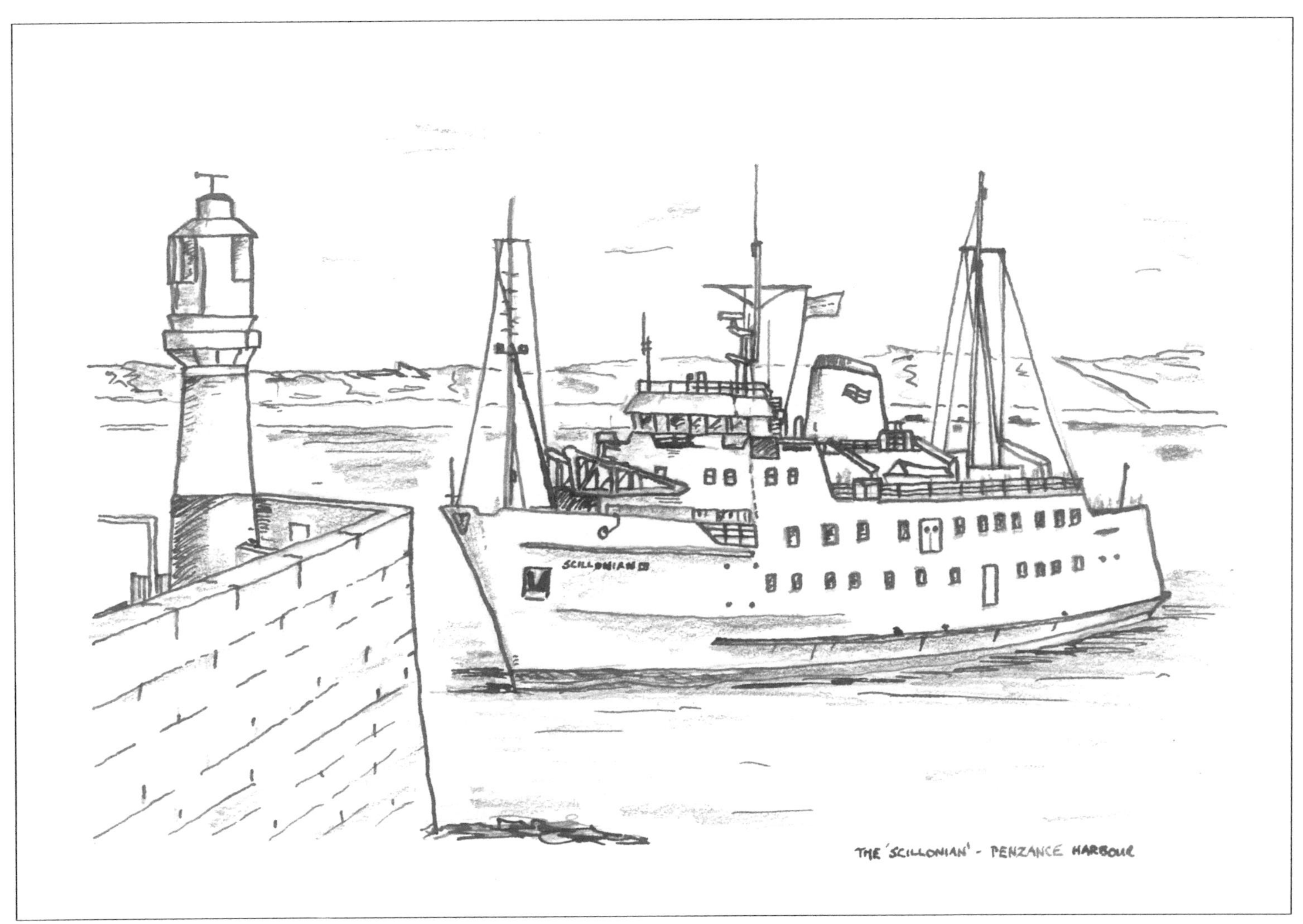

THE 'SCILLONIAN' - PENZANCE HARBOUR

ST. MICHAEL'S MOUNT, MARAZION

Probably the most instantly recognisable place in the United Kingdom after Big Ben, Buckingham Palace, and the Tower of London, St Michael's Mount sits a mile across the ancient granite causeway from the village of Marazion and can only be accessed on foot at low tide.

The castle is the ancestral home of the St. Aubyn family - the Barons St. Levan - and it is well worth the steep climb from the compact harbour for a visit. Quite aside from the grandeur of seeing a castle home, the views across Mount's Bay and down the Lizard Peninsula are a wonder on a clear sunny day…

The castle began life as a monastery in the 12th century and was under the stewardship of the Benedictine order of Mont Saint Michel in Normandy before being captured by Henry La Pomeray in 1193. Later it was held by the Earl of Oxford in the Wars of the Roses in the 15th century. In many ways, it's lucky to survive at all because it held out valiantly as a Royalist stronghold in the English Civil War, and it's a wonder that Cromwell didn't order it to be 'reduced'. Cornwall had been staunchly Royalist in the war and had supplied several regiments in the King's cause. De-militarising such a potent fortress must have been on the Lord Protector's mind!

The island has a small population - around thirty or so - and most have to work or go to school on the mainland. Everyone used to be really jealous of the children on the island who didn't have to go to school if stormy weather and high tides coincided!

One of the occasions I recall going to the Mount was with the Penzance Youth Wind Band to play an afternoon concert on a baking summer's afternoon. I remember having to lug a tuba over the causeway - and what an effort it was!!! At least the heavy wooden case could have doubled as a boat if the tides had not been favourable for the return trip!

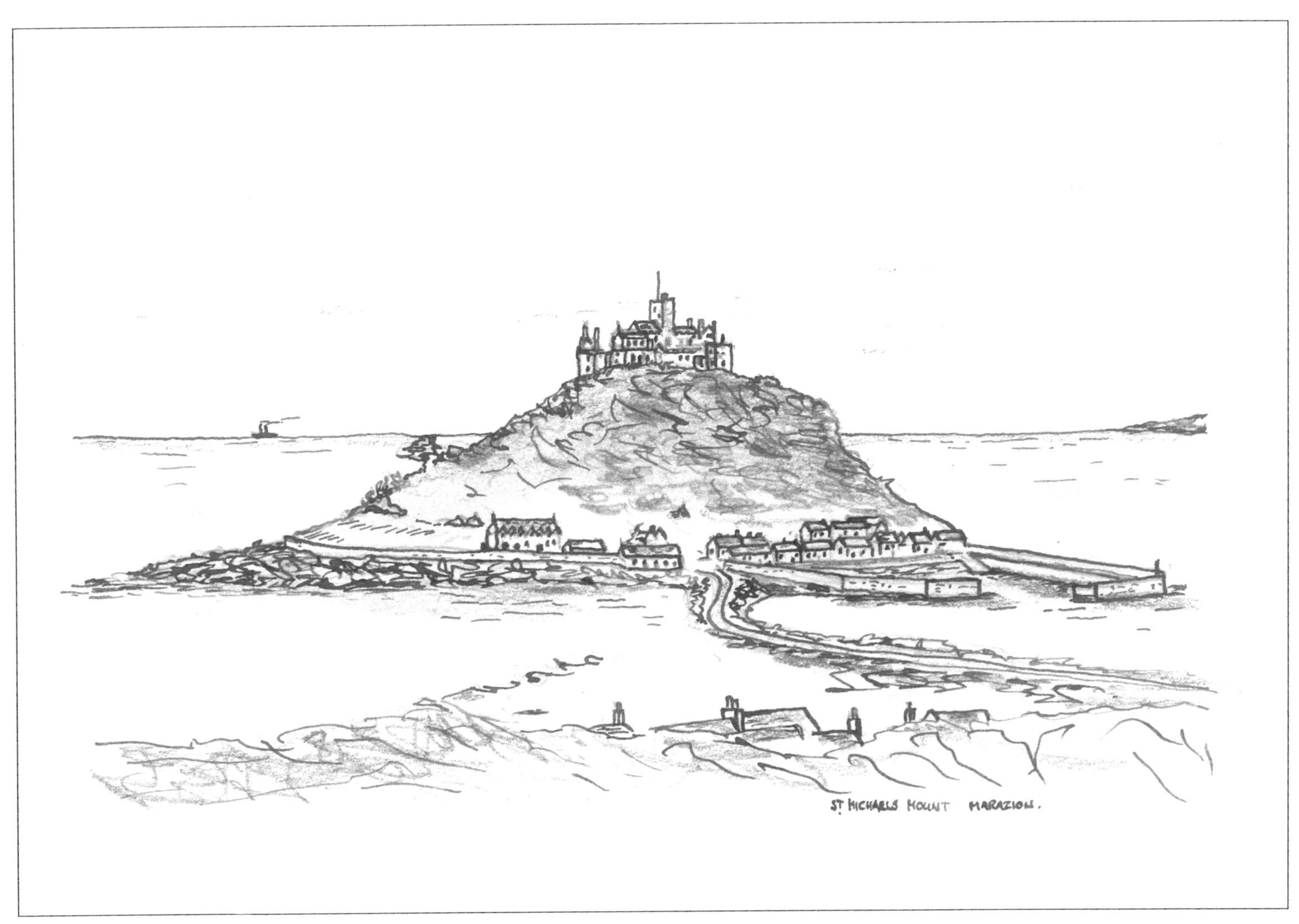

ST MICHAELS MOUNT MARAZION.

AFTERWORD: WHERE ALWAYS SHINES THE SUN

The sun shines always here,
In every day of thought,
Of memories, sights and sounds,
Of tangs and whiffs of salt.

The breeze is gentle, the suns are mild,
The sea is cold and sharp,
The keening of the wheeling birds,
Clear shrieks upon the kelp.

The waves that roar, and boats that grumble,
The doorway chatter loud,
Their accents weathered, laughter soft,
And echoing from the shroud.

Yet far away in passed years,
The sights are clear and strong,
So too the sounds of local voice,
Uplift in Cornish song.

Of brass bands on the West Pier,
Of pasties, Hart's ice cream,
And surfing Porthmeor's breakers,
How far and distant seem.

Forever shall it be for me,
As years recede from sight,
But always with a closed eye,
Such things are rich and bright…..

GBS 2022

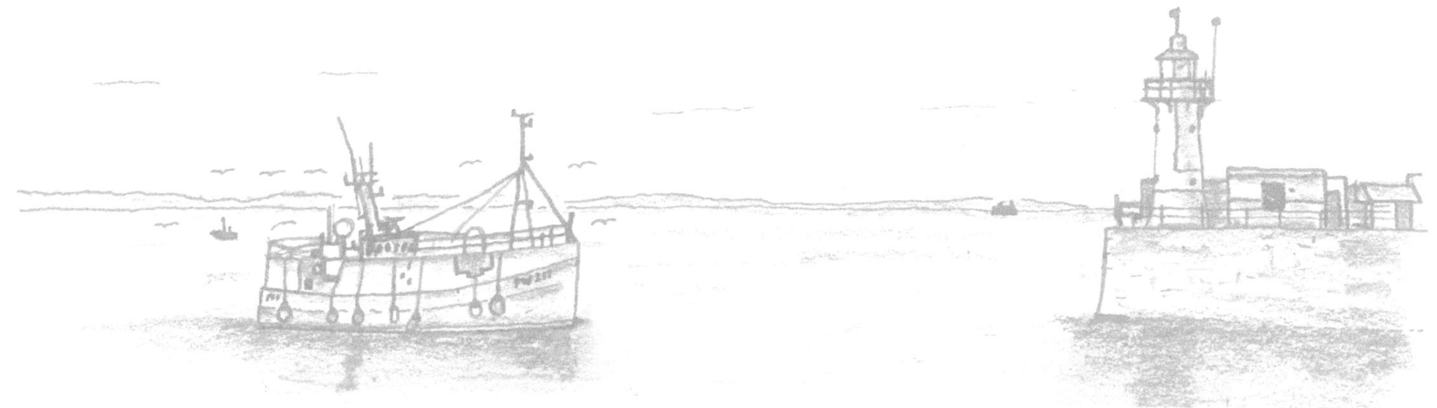

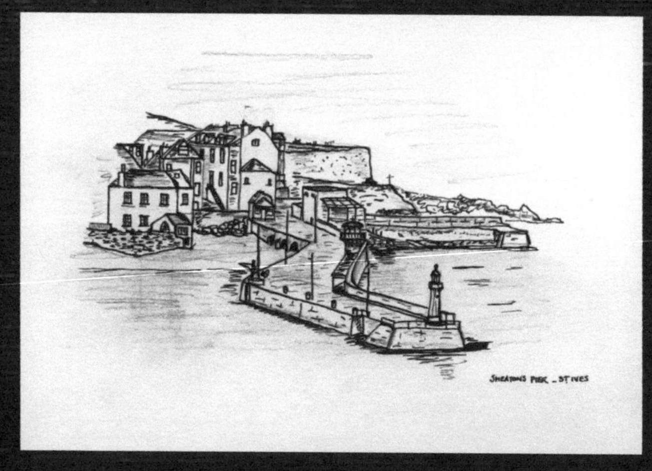

CORNISH SKETCHBOOK

www.pippawhittaker.art